D1645458

PARIAH: COLIN STAGG

COLIN STAGG WITH TED HYNDS

PARIAH:
COLIN STAGG

FOREWORD BY NICK ROSS

Pennant Books

First published in hardback 2007
by Pennant Books

Text copyright © Colin Stagg and Ted Hynds 2007
Edited by Paul Woods

British Library Cataloguing-in-Publication Data:
A catalogue record for this book is available from
The British Library

ISBN 978-1-906015-10-7

Design & Typeset by Envy Design Ltd

Pennant Books
A division of Pennant Publishing Ltd
PO Box 5675
London W1A 3FB

www.pennantbooks.com

ABOUT THE AUTHORS

COLIN STAGG was born in Fulham, southwest London, in 1963. His family later moved to Roehampton, where he has been resident ever since. After being accused of the murder of Rachel Nickell in 1992, he became a national hate figure. He served thirteen months on remand for the crime before an Old Bailey judge ruled he had been unjustly entrapped. But his stigmatisation had only just begun. In the light of recent forensic developments, Colin Stagg has requested that the Metropolitan Police perform a DNA test that will finally exonerate him. Thus far, they have declined to do so. *Pariah* is his personal story.

TED HYNDS formerly ran a top freelance news agency in the West Country. As a Fleet Street journalist in the 1960s, he covered the arrest of Great Train Robber Bruce Reynolds and the disappearance of yachtsman Donald Crowhurst (Ted appears in the award-winning film about the tragedy, *Deep Water*). In the 1980s/90s, he worked at the *Sunday People* and on TV's *The Cook Report*, where he first met Colin Stagg.

I NEVER SAW A WILD THING SORRY FOR ITSELF.
A SMALL BIRD WILL DROP FROZEN DEAD FROM A BOUGH,
WITHOUT EVER HAVING FELT SORRY FOR ITSELF.

DH Lawrence

ACKNOWLEDGEMENTS

Keith Pedder, Ray Levine, Mike Alsford, Alex Tribick,
Kirsty Armstrong, David Canter, Paul Woods, Lee Ashley.
Dave Alford who first brought us together and
Elaine who kept us focused.

FOREWORD
BY NICK ROSS

Public opinion is not always the best, or most subtle, arbiter of criminal guilt or innocence. In fact, the more notorious the crime and the greater the clamour, the more the hot breath of popular sentiment should be resisted. Every now and then there is a witch-hunt based on rumour or media speculation (think of how the McCanns were pilloried after their daughter Madeleine went missing in Portugal), or on occasion Middle England may become convinced someone is innocent when there are compelling reasons to convict (such as the case of Barry George, sentenced for the murder of Jill Dando).

Over almost a quarter of a century working behind the scenes on criminal inquiries – and seeing what does not get published – I have become cautious about making assumptions based on partial reports from newspapers or TV. Nor can I accept that the courts always get the answer right. (How could they, with usually imperfect evidence filtered through their arcane rules?) There have also been times when I was convinced that dangerous people had been acquitted.

But the case of Colin Stagg is one where enough facts are now known, and I am clear that he was not the killer he was made out to be. In fact, of all the thousands of *Crimewatch* appeals I presented, his was the only case that made me worry we had contributed toward an injustice. One key witness named him while we were on the air, and at first there were compelling reasons to suspect him. But the evidence that later emerged shows persuasively that this was a classic story of the wrong man trapped in a horrible web of intrigue. Stagg really was innocent as charged.

October 2007

ONE

My name is Colin Stagg, and I got away with murder. Or at least that's what the police said. And the press. And a lot of people in the street.

It doesn't matter that I was cleared at the Old Bailey. Or that DNA evidence indicates a homicidal maniac as the real killer. I even passed two lie detector tests and submitted to a truth drug. But in the public's mind I was – and still am – guilty.

The life I had enjoyed was stolen from me. I might have seemed like 'lowlife' in many people's eyes, but my life had been my own and I'd liked it. Now, I have no idea how it might have turned out, but I do know it wouldn't have been full of fear, sordid sexual encounters and a disastrous marriage – all minutely chronicled in miles of newsprint.

For years I've been one of the most hated men in Britain. It used to get me down, but not anymore. Now I think of myself as an accident victim. One of those unlucky people who happen to be in the wrong place at the wrong time, and get hit by a truck.

You get bashed up; go into rehab; get better, and come out with a few scars. You lock up the bad memories, throw away the key, and never expect anything good to happen. That way you never get disappointed.

That's how I cope now.

It was a Christmas card that confirmed my outlook, because it came close to killing me.

I'd recognised the writing on the envelope, and knew there would be nothing merry in the message. It had been the same writer every Christmas for years. His words changed, but it always came down to the same sick sentiments.

I was tempted to rip it up and burn it. But that seemed a coward's way out. So I opened it and read: "Happy Christmas from Rachel – another one she won't see, you murdering bastard. If you ever have children I hope they die of cancer." There were two more of the same from anonymous well-wishers: "Why don't you die murdering scum," and "Yore gonna die screaming."

I tore them up and poured myself a whisky. I felt physically sick and sat down on the couch. That's when everything caught up with me. It was one of those moments when you're forced to take stock of your life. What I saw was dismal, and it could only get worse. I'd never felt so sorry for myself before – and I've since made a pact with myself that I never will again.

I was lying on the couch I shared as a bed with my two dogs for warmth. The living room was the flat's only comfort zone, and it was cold. There was barely enough electricity in the meter to cook dinner. So that meant no lights, fire, or television that night.

Despite being fit and willing to work, I couldn't get a job. After years of trying, my local job centre admitted I was unemployable because of my name. So I had to exist on £45 per week dole money. My only luxuries were a few cigarettes and a small bottle of the cheapest whisky.

I was thirty-nine years old. Jobless, penniless, and divorced. With the exception of one brother, I was estranged from my family. Except for my one true friend, there was nobody who cared if I lived or died.

Lying there all alone, I started sobbing. Then howling. The vicious words on the cards had tipped me over the edge. I had endured years of abuse. Spat upon. Sworn at. Punched. Too scared to travel on public transport, or go down the pub.

Not much to show for a life. Not for the first time, I considered ending it. I'd read about looking into the Abyss, and the Abyss looking back into you. I'd never believed it until that moment. Lying there in the dusk that evening, I was at my lowest ebb.

It was the injustice that got to me. I knew I was an innocent man – I'd been cleared of murder, and the police's case against me was discredited by an Old Bailey judge.

But for over a decade I'd been portrayed as a sick, murderous weirdo. That public perception made my life a living hell. If I'd lived in earlier times, I've no doubt I would have been lynched long before.

I don't know how long I lay there, full of self-pity. I knew my ex had left a load of Valium behind when she moved out, and I was so tempted to wash them down with the last of the whisky and end it all . . .

Only the satisfaction it would give my enemies stopped me. The thought of all those smug bastards reading the news, cackling into their cornflakes, held me back.

I had a proud name, and I wasn't going to disgrace it. It might have been a lot easier if I'd changed my name and moved away. But I loved being a Stagg, and I loved my home. It was my fortress and nobody was going to drive me out. I remembered reading once how, in the Middle Ages, the stag had been a symbol of power and loyalty. The more I thought about it the more it gave me strength, and I was determined to stay true to myself, however much I had to endure.

I realised I could cope with being a pariah. I'd had years of practice and the experience hadn't killed me. I've since come to detest self-pity. In my situation it's always a temptation, but, like drugs, it's one I've rejected.

That one bitter night, when it all got on top of me, was a real test. And I passed, in the end. It doesn't do any good to whimper, "Why me, God?" What's *he* going to do to help? I believe in the 'shit happens' philosophy. It was all up to me. There was no one else to deal with it.

Yet it could all have been so very different. I often think back to the day my life changed forever, and wonder about all the little things I could have done to save myself years of misery. With hindsight, I can see how the very slightest difference might have had far-reaching implications.

Every little thing I did or didn't do that day comes back to haunt me. I replay it over and over again in my mind. I can understand how the Greeks and other ancient peoples came to believe so strongly in the Gods, who amused themselves by interfering in human lives.

And how small, seemingly insignificant events can combine to devastating effect, and produce a thunderbolt out of a clear blue sky.

In the months and years that followed, my disrupted life would lead me to meet Professor David Canter, the renowned criminal profiling expert. There's a quote by him that makes me think of everything that was about to happen: "Crime is always a coincidence. People and places come together in a dangerous juxtaposition to create the circumstances for the crime.

"Perhaps more than with any other human interaction, the

element of chance is key. A few minutes or some yards one way or the other and the crime might never have happened."

July 15th 1992 would be one such day – both for the unfortunate victim of a crime, and for me. I woke up as usual, about 6am, to a beautiful summer morning. I had just turned twenty nine, and my body was starting to recover from months of illness.

A crippling bout of coeliac stomach disorder, with its cramps and diarrhoea, had knocked the stuffing out of me. I lost almost two stone in one week, and for months I'd been as weak as a kitten. It left me looking gaunt and haggard, but I felt I was on the mend at last. I'd started using weights again to build up my body and was beginning to get my strength back.

There wasn't too much wrong with my life, or so it seemed to me, except that I'd awoken with a headache. It was something that rarely happened – an omen maybe, but of course I never recognised it as such.

Then, as now, my needs were a lot less than most people's. I hadn't got a proper job, but I earned a few extra pounds doing odd jobs, gardening and a paper round to supplement my dole money.

It doesn't sound much, but it got me out in the open air and, until my stomach problems, kept me very healthy. I'm not very big – only five foot seven – but I've always tried to keep myself in shape, partly because I hoped it would make some woman fancy me.

I had signed on about seven years earlier, when my father became seriously ill. My mother had walked out years before, so there was only me to look after him. He and I were very close. There was high unemployment at the time and someone like me, who had left school with no qualifications, was never likely to find a decent job.

Over the years I've educated myself, like a lot of working-class people did in the early part of the last century. When I was nineteen I applied to join the RAF. I'd passed the initial entry tests, and only needed to attend a final assessment and medical, when my dad had his second heart attack. That was why I dropped the idea, to care for him. It's a pity though, as I think I would have done well in the services.

At the time two of my brothers, Peter and Lee, were still living at home. But they were already into drugs, which I hate, and I couldn't trust them to look after him properly. When he finally died, in 1986, I took over the tenancy and kicked them out. I couldn't stand the drug scene and I haven't seen Peter since.

Female company was the only thing missing from my life. As a teenager I had been painfully shy and not very good-looking. I was always embarrassed about my snaggle teeth and never knew what to say to girls.

My interests were a lot more bookish than most boys on the estate. Although I wasn't 'academic' at school, I read a lot and listened to the news instead of going down the pub and getting pissed.

I was interested in history and nature in all its forms, and I loved animals. These things aren't exactly enthralling conversation topics for teenage girls on a tough council estate. Despite these failings I managed to have a few girlfriends, but they never lasted very long. In a fumbling way I found out about sex, and enjoyed what little I had. But I never had the full Monty!

The closest I'd come to it was in the previous year, 1991, when I started a relationship with a local woman named Tina. She was gorgeous, down-to-earth and sexy. I found I could talk easily to her, and that made all the difference. I lost my shyness

It only lasted a couple of months, and although we didn't have full sex we enjoyed heavy petting. It was my first truly satisfying sexual experience. When she dropped me – to become a policewoman, of all things – shortly before my long illness, I was devastated. I think that was what triggered my stomach problems. I was lovesick.

Like a lot of things in my life, I came to terms with living without sex. Don't get me wrong, I was – and still am – a red-blooded male. But I realised there were other things in life, and I was prepared to settle for them.

So in that summer of '92 I was still a virgin, and resigned to staying that way. But life wasn't so bad. I was always happy with my own company, and I had my dog, Brandy, to lavish affection on. There was work of sorts and, during my recent illness, I'd started thinking about passing my driving test and getting a job as a local delivery driver. It would have got me off the dole and given me independence.

Since kicking my druggie brothers out of the house, I'd lived by myself. If it wasn't a palace it was still my castle. It meant a lot to me.

Not surprisingly, I didn't have any real friends. I knew a lot of people on the estate to say 'hello' to, and I was always courteous and friendly. Although I was very much a loner, I lived quite happily in my own little world with my books, my music and my faithful dog. They were all the company I needed.

Sadly, that was to play a big part in what was to happen to me.

On a rough estate like Roehampton the pack mentality is always there, just below the surface, waiting to strike out, just like you see it in the wild. The pack is quick to turn on the weak or the solitary member. It's ugly but it's understandable.

I've seen it since myself on TV, with suspected paedophiles hounded out of their homes by mobs of screaming, self-righteous women, who probably beat their kids and get beaten in turn by their old man. If I'd been a bloke like that – a drunken bully or a petty crook, even a drug dealer – I would have fitted in. Maybe then the mob wouldn't have turned on me.

But that morning the only cloud on my horizon was a headache. The sun was shining when I walked round to the newsagent, Navnit Patel, to collect the papers for my round, with Brandy trotting along beside me.

After the delivery I went home for breakfast, then decided to take the dog for his usual morning walk. There was no way of knowing, of course, but it was to be the most crucial decision of my life.

My headache had become worse, and I was tempted to take some Paracetamol and sleep it off. But it was a lovely day and, as my recent illness had kept me indoors a lot, I thought the fresh air would do me good. If only I'd given in to the pain and gone to sleep. Life would have been very different.

It was about 8.15 when I set off. I couldn't be exactly sure of the time that morning – or any other – because I'd never owned a watch. The only concession to the headache was my decision not to go too far before coming back to rest.

I was dressed very casually in blue jeans, black cut off T-shirt and white trainers. I was also wearing my black leather motorcycle jacket because it was still early, a bit fresh, and I was still recovering from my illness.

Brandy and I ambled the couple of hundred yards down to Roehampton Lane, crossing over onto the first part of Wimbledon Common. We strolled past the pretty little Scio pond and up to the underpass, below the main A3 Portsmouth Road, which led onto the main part of the common.

It was a lovely morning but my headache was getting worse, so I decided to cut the walk short. We just wandered slowly around the big pond beside the main road, then back to the underpass and home.

I don't suppose we walked more than a mile all told, and got back sometime just after nine, perhaps 9.15. I can't be exact because my head was throbbing, all I wanted to do was make a cup of tea, take some pills and lie down.

What I can remember was that I had time to settle down on the sofa before some daytime quiz programme came on about 9.25. Soon after that I dozed off.

It was the sound of helicopters flying low overhead that woke me, about eleven. I didn't take that much notice of the choppers – they always seemed to be flying low over our estate. My headache was almost gone and I felt a lot better. I thought I'd make it up to Brandy by taking him for a longer walk this time.

It was my second life-changing decision of the day.

After a quick wash to freshen up I changed out of my jeans, as it was much warmer by now. I pulled on a pair of white shorts and a clean white T-shirt, then headed back to the common. I was still wearing my trainer boots and white athletic socks.

This time we walked further down the A3 and crossed through the Putney Vale underpass by the big cemetery. As we walked through the subway, I spotted a policeman at the other end. Brandy was off the lead and wandered past him, onto the grass. The officer stopped me as I attempted to follow my dog, asking if I intended to go onto the common. I thought it was a daft question – that was obviously what I was about to do – but he was so pleasant about it that I couldn't take offence.

When I confirmed that was where I was heading, he told me there had been 'an incident'. Naturally I asked him what had happened, and he added, "I suppose you'll know sooner or later – a girl's body has been found."

That shook me. All I could say was, "Where?" He pointed generally towards the common and replied, "Somewhere over there, by some hills."

I assumed he meant a little girl's body had been found, which indicated she'd been murdered. What I did next made perfect sense at the time. My natural instinct was to be helpful, so I said I'd been on the common earlier that morning with my dog. That proved to be a big mistake.

He asked what time, and I said between about 8.30 and 9.15. I couldn't be more exact. I told him I hadn't heard or seen anything suspicious, and provided him with my name and address when requested.

Then I collected Brandy, turned round and went back the way I came. Of course, I was a bit excited about what he'd told me. Although I didn't know exactly where it had taken place, it was in an area where I'd walked every day for years. So when I popped into my local butcher's shop to buy some mincemeat for lunch on the way home, I wanted to talk about it.

I had come to know Pat Heanen well. He was always chatty and friendly. Sometimes he would give me little off-cut treats for Brandy. It was only natural to tell him about what I understood to be a little girl's murder, except that I used the words 'young girl'. It was a really good bit of gossip.

He wanted to know how I knew, so I told him about the policeman at the underpass. At that he called over his assistant, Les, who said he'd seen police on the common earlier and thought they were looking for a lost kid. That tied in with what I thought was a little girl's murder.

After buying my mincemeat, I went into the newsagent's next door to tell Navnit Patel. He wasn't there but his son Yagnesh was. In what was to become my opening remark most of that day, I said, "Have you heard about the common? They've found a young girl's body." The news must have spread like wildfire because he said his father had already told him. With that, Brandy and I headed home.

As we arrived on the balcony outside my front door I met Peter Witt, one of my neighbours, and went through the 'have you heard?' ritual again.

After a few minutes' chat, I went in to cook my lunch and left Brandy sprawled asleep outside in the sun. I should have left him there. But when I finished eating I thought I'd take him for another walk, to make up for the one he'd missed earlier.

That was how I came to bump into Lillian Avid, a silly old woman I'd met about a year earlier, out walking her dog. Once more I gave her the 'Have you heard what happened on the common?' greeting. Her response was really strange. "Oh, murdered was she? Are you sure you didn't do it?"

I got indignant and told her not to be so daft. With that she changed the subject, and said I was looking very fit and well. I thought she was referring to my months of illness, and agreed that I was much better.

I didn't see her again until about three weeks later, when I bumped into her and her dog. We got talking about the murder, and I mentioned that I'd heard on the news they were looking for a man with a ponytail. She amazed me by grabbing her own hair and saying, "Well it couldn't be me, because I don't have a ponytail!"

She wasn't joking, and I remember thinking she must be going senile. But when she asked me if I'd accompany her walking her dog across the common, because she was scared to do so alone, I readily agreed. She was, after all, a little old lady.

I carried on walking across the common with my dog like I'd done every day for years. As far as I could tell from the TV and the papers, this murder hunt was still big news. But it seemed to be getting nowhere.

How wrong I was!

The killing, as I came to realise, had touched the heart of the nation like nothing since the Moors Murders, nearly thirty years before.

The victim was a stunningly beautiful young mum, Rachel

Nickell. She was just twenty-three, and nobody could fail to be moved by the family video film of her playing with her little son, Alex. The slim blonde seemed to radiate happiness off the screen. In fact the photo of her smiling, carefree face has become iconic, instantly recognisable today, more than fifteen years on.

What also burned her image into people's minds was the way she died. Literally butchered in front of her two-year-old baby boy, on a bright summer morning, within shouting distance of dozens of walkers.

I can understand why I became such a hate figure – because for years, I was regarded as the man who got away with murdering this lovely young woman. As an innocent man, I felt victimised. Looking back, I can see I wasn't the only one.

Her death ultimately ruined a lot of lives and careers. Everyone involved in the case was scarred by it. Her family, her partner, their son, the murder squad and their advisers, all suffered in some way. Some left their jobs or lost their reputations as a direct result of the case. It was one of the most horrific crimes of all time. For me, it also became one of the all-time police cock-ups.

Right from the start, you knew it was going to be one of those cases where the police were under massive pressure to get a conviction. This wasn't some sordid drug death or a lovers' tiff gone bad. Rachel was an idealised vision of youth, beauty and motherhood. An ex-army officer's daughter, raised in a loving upper-middle class family, deeply in love with her partner and their baby son.

Not only Middle England but the whole of British public opinion demanded the monster responsible be brought to justice. The quicker, the better.

It was also meat and drink to the animals of our national press. Brown paper envelopes full of cash ensured a steady stream of leaks from the investigation squad. Almost every new lead quickly found its way into the papers. The press pack was in full cry, baying for blood and headlines.

As I would discover later, through reading witness statements, the full horror was first revealed at 10.35am, when Rachel's mutilated body was found under a silver birch tree beside a woodland path by dog walker Michael Murray.

She had been stabbed forty nine times in a violent, uncontrolled, sustained attack. As she died, or immediately afterwards, the killer rammed the knife hilt up her bottom in a perverted sex act. Such ferocious force had gone into the attack that every major organ in her body was damaged. One thrust was so fierce that the hilt of the knife's outline was imprinted onto her flesh.

It all happened less than three hundred yards from the busy Windmill café car park on Wimbledon Common, within an incredibly short timeframe. Only fifteen minutes had passed since mother and son had been spotted by cyclist Roger McKern at 10.20, walking their little black and white dog, Molly, along a path through the trees, heading slowly towards the killing ground.

Forensic experts estimated the frenzied attack lasted no more than three to four minutes. From her wounds, they deduced the first blow had been to her outstretched palm. Two small chest cuts indicated he prodded her backwards, further into the copse, before slashing her larynx, effectively silencing any calls for help.

The dying woman was forced to her knees while he commenced a stabbing frenzy, twenty-six blows to her front and another nineteen from behind, with a further three to her neck and the slash to her left hand.

This horror was inflicted in a very short space of time. From Mr Murray's line of sight, and the direction from which he was walking, the killer must have left by 10.32 at the latest to avoid being spotted. So between then and Mr McKern's last sighting was a matter of about twelve minutes. And at the ambling pace Rachel was walking at, the attack couldn't have started until about 10.23.

That left at most a nine-minute window of opportunity, on a well-used path only yards from an open space where mothers and children were playing. Yet incredibly, nobody heard or saw a thing.

For Mr Murray, an elderly retired architect, it was a nightmarish scene. Rachel's blood-soaked corpse was curled up in a foetal position, with her little boy clinging to it, begging, "Get up, Mummy, get up." She has been almost beheaded by a blow which slit her throat from ear to ear. Her jeans and underwear had been dragged down to her ankles, leaving her naked and vulnerable from the waist down.

It may have been that Murray's arrival saved the child's life. Bruising on the little boy's cheek confirmed what he told them about trying to stop the man "hurting Mummy" and being knocked away into some brambles. Detectives believe the killer may have planned to remove the only eyewitness until he heard someone approaching and fled.

Shocked almost out of his senses by what he found, Murray managed to prise the child's fingers from the body. Then, carrying the traumatised little boy, he stumbled through light undergrowth to a patch of open ground less than twenty feet away, where he had spotted a group of young mothers and children.

After gently handing the mud and blood-spattered boy to Emma Brooks, who was out for a walk with her two kiddies and their dog, he went for help. Alex kept whimpering, "I want my mummy, I want my mummy . . . I'm cold . . . I'm tired."

Mrs Brooks ran back to her friend Penny Horne, trying to comfort the distraught child. Mrs Horne wrapped him in her baby's shawl for warmth. At that moment the women spotted jogger Sean Beckett, who was quickly sent for help. Within minutes he had met mounted ranger Stephen Francis, who rode back to the frightened mothers.

"I think there's a body over there in the bushes," Mrs Brooks told him. He dismounted and entered the wooded area, where he almost immediately found Rachel's corpse. He realised at once there was nothing he could do to help. The throat wound alone was obviously fatal, so he backed off to preserve the crime scene.

By now news of the murder was spreading. As the first police arrived, frightened mums were dragging their children back to the car park and off the common. More and more officers swarmed onto the scene. Some started taping off the murder site while others tried to collect witness statements.

They were quickly given an important clue by a woman named Amanda Phelan. About 10.40 she had seen a man apparently washing his hands in a drainage ditch, not far from where the body was discovered. He had aroused her suspicions as she approached by ducking down into the little stream and scrubbing his hands. He then walked off in the direction of Putney Vale Cemetery – where my dad is buried. Her description of this man was thought to be of great importance by the police.

She said he was in his late twenties or early thirties and about six feet tall, but she couldn't get a good look at him because he kept his head down. He was wearing light blue trousers or jeans with a cream or white sweater, and carrying a black bag. After noticing her looking at him, he hurried off in the direction of the cemetery, towards the main road and our estate.

Later, her dogs started barking when she passed some bushes by the graveyard wall. She was sure someone was hiding there. This seemed probable when police searched the area and tracker dogs followed a scent from the drainage ditch to the wall. Like so many subsequent accounts from witnesses on or near the common that day, the suspect's clothing was to play a vital – and sometimes misleading – role.

One witness who was to have a big impact on my life was solicitor's wife Jane Harriman. She was stopped and questioned by police as she left the common with her seven-year-old daughter and three young sons, aged thirteen, eleven and three. A man had aroused her suspicions on three occasions between 10.10 and 10.23, close to the murder scene. She and her children were invited to Wimbledon police station to give the first of three statements. Her description was of a man in his late twenties or early thirties, with a thin, babyish face, who walked with a slight but distinctive stoop.

She told police: "He was white, about five ten-ish tall. He had close cropped hair, darkish brown. On the top half of his body he was wearing a white shirt. It was long sleeved with a collar. He was wearing dark coloured trousers.

"I cannot remember what colour they were or what material they were made of. His shirt was tucked into his trousers. He was carrying a dark coloured bag.

"At that point, apart from his shirt and trousers, there was nothing else on his body. The bag he had was a dark colour. I couldn't be sure what material it was made of, but some sort of vinyl I think. From a distance I thought it was a briefcase. But close up it seemed more like a sports bag."

He had first passed Jane Harriman and her children at about 10.10, near the common's Curling Pond, behaving oddly and turning his face away from her. He ignored her 'good morning' and turned his face away.

Seven minutes later she noticed him again, apparently following an attractive blonde who was later identified as a policeman's wife. He was walking briskly now, but nervously, with a slight stoop. Mrs Harriman became concerned for the woman's safety and kept her eye on him. Checking her watch, she saw it was 10.17.

Six minutes later she saw him again, walking around the pond towards a wooded area to her left, where he disappeared through a gap in the trees. The sinister stranger was headed directly towards the murder scene. On this last sighting he was wearing what appeared to be a thin belt or strap round his waist, over his shirt.

Her evidence came to be regarded by the police as vital. Over the next two months she retraced her route for a police video crew and helped compose a photofit picture of the man she had seen. This was shown on the September 1992 *Crimewatch* programme. It was to have massive repercussions for me, both then and for the foreseeable future.

By mid-morning there was a heavy police presence on and around the common, as the murder investigation moved into action. At its height it was to involve over a hundred officers.

Rachel had been identified through the registration number of her silver Volvo estate, which had been left in the Windmill car park shortly before she set off on her fateful walk. Her merchant banker brother Mark was contacted at his City office, but her parents were on holiday in America and could not be reached. Unable to contact her partner, Andre Hanscombe, police went to their flat in Balham, four miles away, where a flatmate let them in. It was there, about midday, that Andre called home, expecting to say hello to Rachel and Alex. Instead, he was answered by a police officer who gave him the dreadful news.

His response was to sit down on the kerb and howl like a wounded animal. When I heard about it, my heart went out to him. I've subsequently howled my guts out – but that was me feeling sorry for myself, not mourning the loss of my loved one. I can't even imagine how I would react to heartbreaking news like that.

Andre then accompanied police to the hospital where Alex had been taken for attention to the cuts and bruises on his face. In an emotional reunion for father and son, he had to explain in the gentlest terms that Mummy had had an accident and would not be coming home with them.

Then, while Alex slept, the detectives began their detailed questioning of Andre to learn everything they could about Rachel Jane Nickell.

TWO

Rachel was the woman who literally turned my life upside down. We never met, but since her death we've become inseparable. Our two names are linked forever, like Beauty and the Beast.

Over the years I've come to know a lot about her, from the police and press reports. I think she was the sort of person everybody would have wanted to know — although I doubt if she would have wanted to know someone like me.

Our backgrounds were so very different. She had been born into a well-to-do family in the little Essex village of Great Totham, near Colchester, on November 23rd 1968. After a long army career, which saw him rise to the rank of major, her father Andrew retired and built up a successful shoe import business. Rachel and her elder brother Mark were brought up in a secure and loving family. She attended the local primary school and won an eleven-plus place at Colchester High, the local grammar school.

According to her teachers she was a model pupil, sailing through her exams and collecting ten O-levels and three A-levels in English, History and Law. She excelled at sports, particularly swimming, and had a natural talent for song and dance and amateur dramatics.

Outside school she was equally talented, a star of the Essex Dance Theatre in Chelmsford, where the principal was reported as saying, "She could easily have made it in the West End. She had the ability and the looks and she passed all her exams with ease.

"This was a girl who had everything going for her and was going places. It's tragic to think so much talent has gone to waste."

Offers of modelling work came while she was only fifteen, but on her parents' advice she turned them down to concentrate on her studies. After leaving school, she began a degree course in English and history and a promising future seemed assured. She moved to Plumstead in southeast London – which I think may have been of great significance, as I'll explain later – and worked out-of-term as a part-time model and lifeguard to fund her studies.

It was while working at Richmond Baths in August 1988 that she met the love of her life, as she was breaking up with another man. Andre Hanscombe was an olive-skinned, twenty-four-year-old motorcycle courier, and a handsome bloke. He had been a professional tennis coach and was working as a dispatch rider to pay for a little two-bedroom flat he'd bought in Elmfield Road, Balham. He swept her off her feet and they quickly became inseparable. Rachel, still only nineteen, moved in with him a few months later. Despite being on the pill, she soon became pregnant and was forced to put her degree on hold shortly before the birth of little Alex, in August 1989. Rachel took to motherhood easily and adored her new baby. She took him to mother and baby swimming sessions at the nearby Balham Leisure Centre, to pass on her own love of the water. They were also frequent visitors to her parents' new home in Ampthill, Bedfordshire where Monica and Andrew Nickell doted on their adored grandson.

Life seemed to be smiling on the young lovers, but they were finding it hard to make ends meet, and were forced to take in lodgers to help pay the mortgage. They had been discussing moving out of London to the countryside, or possibly France, where Andre could pursue his tennis-coaching career. But the slump in property prices forced them to put this idea on hold as they continued to have money worries.

And in the months before her murder, Rachel's normal bubbly moods became darker. It was as if she had some terrible premonition of what was to happen to her. Andre described her depression as a 'black hole', but it was a succession of horrific nightmares in the months before her murder that deeply upset them both.

Since the murder Andre has held an almost pathological hatred for me, which I've always tried to excuse. He may be surprised to find me quoting from his own book, *The Last Thursday in July*, but I think it's valuable:

"At times Rachel had the most horrific and vivid nightmares. Always involving something awful and bloody happening to her.

"Once she sat bolt upright in bed in the middle of the night. I woke up straight away. 'Why did you do that to me?' she asked, looking straight at me . . .

"Rachel's expression was that of someone bitterly betrayed. It turned my stomach to lead.

"'Why did you kill me?' she said. I realised she must have been having a nightmare. In fact I could see that was actually still asleep."

Were her bad dreams a chilling warning? Some psychic premonition of violent death? Or just a manifestation of the domestic worries preying on her mind? Having since experienced dreams myself that foretold of people's deaths, I believe Rachel had terrible premonitions of her murder.

One of my strangest experiences came when I was washing up one morning. It suddenly came into my head that an old lady I knew had died. I shrugged it off, but later that day I met a neighbour who knew her, and I asked how she was. "Oh, haven't you heard? She had a heart attack this morning and died," she replied.

And about a month before Rachel's death, I was standing on a hillock close to what would be the murder scene, watching a beautiful sunset with my dog. It was a peaceful setting, but suddenly I got this horrible sensation. It felt like something was going to take all this beauty away from me, and it made me hurry on home.

For a few days after that I couldn't sleep properly. But I had a dream that one of my brothers, Lee, had escaped from prison and wanted me to go abroad with him. In my dream we went to Spain. Perhaps I should have heeded the warning.

But in Rachel's life, whatever her forebodings, she still presented that beautiful sunny smile to the world. However down she felt, it didn't effect her doting on Alex. Sharing walks on nearby Tooting Bec Common was a pleasure for them both – until about six months before her death, when a man exposed himself to her. Andre made her report the incident to the police, and after that she switched their walks to Wandsworth Common.

But after being pestered by another man, she made the fateful decision to drive the extra few miles to leafy Wimbledon. She went there three or four times a week through that early spring and summer, giving Alex fresh air and their little dog plenty of exercise. There, among the dozens of young mums, dog walkers and cyclists in a traditional London greenspace, she understandably felt safe. Tragically, she was wrong.

This golden girl's life was snuffed out under a silver birch tree on a woodland path, within shouting distance of a busy car park, with her traumatised little boy looking on. Her murder caused nationwide revulsion and a growing demand for the police to catch her killer. And, after two months of intense investigation, they finally found their prime suspect. Me.

I still don't fully understand why they picked me out. At best they only had some anecdotal evidence that may or may not have put me on the common before the murder. The most charitable explanation I can give is that the police were under so much pressure that they clutched at straws. The uncharitable view is that they needed a 'result' at any price, and I was the one who paid.

Up until that fateful summer, I had led a quiet, uneventful and – truth be told – boring life. The second of five children, I was born in May 1963 in Fulham, southwest London. It was a squalid area to grow up in. My dad was a bill poster and my mum had various part-time jobs to support the growing family.

My early childhood memories are happy ones, although from the start I was a bit different from my brothers and sister. I was always very shy and quiet, unlike the rest of them.

When I was five, we moved to the maisonette in Roehampton where I still live, close to Wimbledon Common and Richmond Park. In those days it was on a nice new estate, nothing like the sinkhole housing it later became. Dad was pleased because we had a garden at last, and we kids loved it because the common was so close for us to play on.

The whole family would often go over to the ponds or up to the famous Windmill for picnics. So we got to know the area very well from a young age. My dad used to take Rex, the family dog, for walks across there every day. That's how I inherited my love of the common, I used to keep him company and we enjoyed walking and talking.

I don't remember too much, but my impression is that it was a happy time – although we didn't have much money and there were five little kids crammed into a small three-bedroom flat. I do remember that my dad did most of the domestic jobs. In addition to going out to work, he did a lot of the cooking and cleaning and shopping.

Then, after twenty years with the same firm, he was made redundant. I suspect it was because he was devoting so much time to us that his real work suffered. In any case, he was devastated. And soon afterwards it got even worse for him.

I suppose the strain of having such a big young family took its toll on my mother, Hilda, because when I was about eleven she suddenly ran off with her driving instructor. It didn't seem to have much effect on me or my younger brother, Peter, at the time. Perhaps that was when I first learnt to bottle up my feelings, to keep from being hurt. But Dad was gutted. A week later, he suffered his first heart attack

Mum wasn't living that far away, so occasionally she would come back to see us at weekends, but that gradually eased off. Social Services tried to have us put into care but Dad wouldn't hear of it. Vic Stagg was an old-fashioned bloke who believed in his family responsibilities. Somehow he scrimped and saved, and even went without food himself, to keep us together.

Then my mother's boyfriend kicked her out, and my father foolishly took her back. But she didn't play happy families for long. She started seeing another man, and this time my dad had had enough humiliation. He let her go and got a divorce. Unusually for the time, he also won custody of us kids, although my mum was granted regular access. She quickly remarried. I remember going round to her new home on Saturday afternoons and not liking it very much. By this time I had just about given up on her, and nothing she's done down the years since has caused me to change my mind.

In the end I had a father whom I hero-worshipped and a mother I despised. The funny thing is that, even though she cheated on her first boyfriend with another instructor, she still can't drive.

Whether it was this family break-up or my own personality, I don't know, but I became more reclusive as I grew into my teens and a lot of my old friends moved away. I loved reading and devoured non-fiction books. This made me seem even more of a loner, I suppose, but I never really thought about it. Of course, I was still interested in a lot of things that other boys were into at that time, particularly kung fu films. That was something that would come back to haunt me.

Like a lot of other kids on the estate I had made some Bruce Lee rice flails, decorating them with Chinese letters for more realism. I was out on my bike with them one day when a police patrol stopped me. I was arrested for having an offensive weapon, and fined at juvenile court. Years later, that incident would be used to indicate I had an unhealthy interest in martial arts, rather than just being some dopey teenager copying the latest fad. But the nunchukas were not even a prank. Never intended for use as a weapon or to harm anyone, they were simply something that youngsters made – like bows and arrows, or wooden swords and catapults, for an earlier generation.

Contrary to a lot of rumours around the estate, and inaccurate press reports, it was my only brush with the law until I was arrested in the Rachel murder inquiry.

The rest of my teenage years passed without incident. Despite my prolific reading, I didn't achieve much at school, although I was very good at art and showed some flair for French. But I left with no qualifications and took a succession of menial jobs.

By this time I'd started to be interested in the girls, but my natural reserve and shyness made it difficult for me. I was self-conscious about my lack of height and looks. I had very little confidence in making conversation, unless it was about history or some other topic I was deeply interested in.

There were a couple of short-lived romances, but nothing serious. It didn't bother me too much because I always believed that, sooner or later, I'd find the right woman and settle down to have a family.

But as the years went by, it just didn't happen and I became resigned to being on my own. I was very lucky in the respect that I enjoyed my own company and didn't have any great expectations. Through helping my dad in his vegetable plot, I discovered a talent for gardening. I started to get small gardening jobs and general handyman work around the estate.

When he died from a second sudden heart attack in 1986, it was a terrible shock. It happened without warning and I couldn't believe that this decent man, who I idolised, was gone in an instant. I was devastated. He gave me my love of the natural world, so I took over his garden and made it flourish as a memorial to him.

But I wasn't so tender towards my brothers. There were only two of them living at home by then and, like so many people on the estate, they were heavily into smoking dope. I've never approved of drugs and, after a short while, I couldn't stand their druggie culture any more and locked them out of the flat, which the council had transferred into my name.

From then on I lived alone – except for my old Labrador cross, Sally, who died in 1990. Soon after that, a neighbour gave me another dog, a crossbreed called Brandy, who became my daily companion on walks across the common.

By then my life had settled into a simple – and, to many people, boring – pattern. It wasn't boring to me, of course. Never having been a follower of fashion, I wasn't interested in flash clothes or a lot of the things that money can buy.

I didn't drink much, because by now I had very few friends. I wasn't into the drink and drug culture that prevailed on the estate, and I hated the local pubs. If I wanted a drink I would buy a bottle and have it at home. As long as I had enough to eat and books to read, I was perfectly happy. I also enjoyed painting and playing the guitar. Never having been an ambitious bloke, I didn't have anything much to strive for.

It might not have been many people's idea of happiness, but to me it was the good life. I still miss its simplicity. I was just a face in the crowd, unexceptional and unnoticed except in a vague sort of way, quietly getting on with my uneventful life.

Unbeknownst to me, all that was to change dramatically.

After the initial flurry of publicity, the police investigation had gone quiet and seemed to be making little progress. What nobody realised was that they had identified almost a hundred potential suspects who had to be interviewed and eliminated.

But despite this frantic behind-the-scenes activity, privately the senior officers must have felt they were not making headway. Worried by the lack of progress, the Association of Chief Police Officers made the fateful recommendation to use a psychological profiler, who might hold the key to identifying Rachel's killer.

The senior investigating officer agreed. And that was how my nemesis, in the shape of Paul Britton, a smug, self-styled 'Cracker', was brought in to help the stalled investigation on July 28th. It was a decision that would make me the prime suspect – ultimately ruining my life, and leading to disgrace and humiliation for most of those involved.

Britton's mistakes may have allowed Rachel's killer to go free to kill again, while making me a monster in the public's eyes. The police weren't blameless either. Although I like to think the lead detectives acted from a genuine desire to catch the killer, their focus settled far too easily on me.

If I still can't forgive them for what they did, over the years I've come to understand their motivation a little better. Heading the murder hunt was Detective Superintendent John 'Bertie' Bassett, a quietly spoken, silver-haired veteran officer, only five months away from retirement. The Nickell inquiry looked like being his last big job and he wanted to leave on a high. He was to be sadly disillusioned.

The senior 'hands-on' officers under him were both ex-Flying Squad men, Chief Inspector Mick Wickerson and Detective Inspector Keith Pedder. They were big, tough blokes with athletic builds. You could imagine them grabbing you by the scruff of the neck and rasping, "You're nicked, son!" in best Regan of the Sweeney-style.

Pedder always seemed to me the more dangerous one. He was an ex-public schoolboy, which he hid behind his bushy macho moustache and laidback manner. But he couldn't hide the intelligence in his eyes, and underneath that softly, softly approach he was as hard as nails. He was also a master of interrogation, who could tie you in knots. As a newly promoted detective inspector – it was the first week in his new job when he was seconded to the Nickell murder – he had a lot to prove. I was to be his ticket to hero status, so it seemed.

At the time, Pedder was in his mid-thirties with seventeen years' experience behind him, and highly regarded. This job was supposed to be the making of him, the express elevator up the greasy promotion pole. Instead, it would break him. In the light of what happened to me, I can't feel too sorry for him. He would find out firsthand what it's like to be an innocent suspect, and how it trashes your life. His experiences mirrored my own in many ways, but I'll let him tell his personal story later.

On the face of it this was an A-team investigation. The top men combined experience, toughness, tenacity and imagination. These weren't shift-work coppers. And the crime itself had been horrific enough to touch them all on an emotional level. DCI Wickerson was almost tearful when he gave the first TV news description of the murder. From what I've been told, the whole squad were similarly affected. Pedder himself has admitted this was the one case – out of the hundreds he investigated – that he would never forget.

Before switching their searchlight onto me, they had quickly hoovered up dozens of potential suspects – and just as quickly spat them out. Their biggest problem was that they were woefully short of hard evidence. The sole eyewitness was a traumatised baby boy, just under three years of age.

The murder scene revealed nothing. The only forensic find was a minute particle of what the science of the day called 'organic matter', taken from the body. (Now it may prove invaluable in finally clearing my name. But at the time it was useless.) The only concrete information lay in the dozens of varied and conflicting statements taken from people walking on the common that morning, and in hundreds of calls to the incident room.

The police trawled their records for details of sex offenders living in, or close to, the area. This produced over a hundred names as potential suspects, all of whom had to be traced, interviewed and eliminated. They were getting snowed under by a blizzard of paperwork and unproductive leads. Their only eventual breakthrough came from little Alex who, thanks to patient and gentle probing by a child psychologist, had started to reveal some details about his mother's killer.

With the use of play therapy and dolls, they gradually built up this small child's view of the murderer. According to Alex, the man was white. He was wearing dark blue trousers – not jeans, as I then wore every day of my life – a white button-up shirt outside his trousers, and a belt over the shirt. His shoes were dark and he was carrying a black bag, from which he produced a knife. The little boy's description matched a hunting knife.

They couldn't be one hundred per cent certain about this evidence, because of Alex's age. But it was at least a starting point. And in certain aspects it matched the evidence of Jane Harriman, who had provided the most compelling sightings of a man acting suspiciously shortly before the murder. Alex also said that "the bad man washed the blood off in the water" after walking away towards the stream. This gave credence to Amanda Phelan's sighting of a man washing his hands in a drainage ditch, close to the murder scene.

These obviously harrowing talks with little Alex also solved one minor mystery. Police had been baffled by a small piece of paper containing Rachel's bank PIN number, which was found on her face. They thought the killer had left it for some bizarre reason. But it turned out that Alex, with his small child's logic, had put it there as a "bandage for Mummy".

Over a period of about a month, the child psychologist coaxed more information from the little boy. He revealed that the man was on foot, did not have a dog with him, and had acted alone. But over time Alex became less responsive, and by the beginning of September they were no further forward.

They had taken in over a dozen potential suspects for questioning without result, other than to accidentally uncover a violent sex offender from Liverpool who was later jailed. Other than the minute piece of 'organic material', there was absolutely no forensic evidence. There was no murder weapon and no useful intelligence on any potential suspect. Despite various sightings of potentially suspicious characters, none had been identified. The investigation was at a dead end.

It took the offer of a slot on BBC1's *Crimewatch* to galvanise the inquiry. They knew that TV coverage on this high-profile programme often encouraged potential witnesses – who would otherwise not bother to come forward. Unlike newspaper stories, this appeal and reconstruction were to be beamed direct into people's homes, which would have a much greater impact. I was soon to find out exactly how much.

The show was to be broadcast on September 17th, and in the preceding weeks the police team concentrated on how to make the most of their appeal to the public. It was decided early on to keep it simple, so as not to confuse people with an avalanche of information. They agreed to reveal Paul Britton's psychological profile, and to ask the public to think along similar lines to his detailed 'portrait' of the killer. This, they hoped, would jog memories, or remind people of some detail that previously seemed unimportant and not worth bringing to police attention.

For the visual impact they decided on screening two of the dozens of E-fits put together from sightings on or near the common, on the morning of the murder. They settled for the man seen by Amanda Phelan washing his hands in the drainage ditch, close to the murder scene.

This was a potentially strong suspect, as Alex had also described how the killer washed in the stream. He was described as about five foot ten tall, in his twenties or early thirties with short brown hair, dressed distinctively with a belt over his white shirt and carrying a black (or dark) bag. He was also remarkably similar to the three sightings of a man acting suspiciously before the murder by Jane Harriman. Finding his identity was crucial.

For some strange reason, the second photofit was of a man they had dubbed the 'A3 runner'. This was based on the sighting of a skinny white male, with long blond or grey-streaked hair, possibly in a ponytail, running up Norstead Place beside the A3, on the edge of the common. All efforts to trace this man had failed. But the witness also described seeing the police helicopter overhead at the time, which made it 11.15 at the earliest – forty-five minutes after the murder.

It still seems unlikely to me that the killer would have remained in the area for so long, but it was their choice. And from their point of view, the screening was a great success. Within hours of the broadcast, the incident room had been swamped by over eight hundred calls in a massive public response. They dealt mainly with possible identities for the two photofits and candidates for Britton's psychological profile of the murderer.

One name stuck out in both of these categories: Colin Francis Stagg. My nightmare had begun.

What excited the police was that several people had identified me as the Harriman suspect, while others said I was a local loner and a bit of a weirdo who fitted the profile. More importantly, I lived nearby and was already in their computer system, after being stopped when I attempted to enter the common after the murder. Within twelve hours I would be under arrest.

On Friday September 18th, my day started as usual with my paper round, then back home for breakfast. About 8.30am I started to walk along the communal balcony, intending to go to the doctor's surgery for a repeat prescription of the special diet food used to treat my stomach illness.

As I did, I noticed Lillian Avid standing by the end of the steps. She was the daft old woman who had asked if it was me who 'did it' on the morning of the murder. She was pretending to be interested in the line of pagan symbols I had painted on my door.

(They signified my own name, decorated with Celtic and mythical figures like Beowulf and Robin Hood.)

But what she really wanted to do was check my address, because she had seen the *Crimewatch* programme and planned to phone the police to say she recognised one of the photofits as me.

She needn't have bothered. As I approached her, two men walked up to us very purposefully. I may not have been very streetwise but, as most people on the estate would have done, I knew instantly they were 'Old Bill'.

One of them motioned me towards them and asked for a 'quiet word'. Then, after confirming who I was, they produced their warrant cards. Detective Constable Paul Miller said, "I'm arresting you on suspicion of the murder of Rachel Nickell. You are not obliged to say anything, but it may harm your defence if you do not mention when questioned something which you later rely on in court."

We've all heard those words a thousand times on the telly. But when it happens to you it's like a punch in the belly. You can't breathe. You can't think. You panic. All I could splutter out was, "I could never do something like that . . . you must be joking." But of course they weren't.

They took me back to my flat and seemed delighted to read the sign on my front door: "Christians Beware: a pagan dwells here." That too would be used against me. I'd put it there as a sort of jokey deterrent, after being pestered by Jehovah's Witnesses. One more little prank that backfired on me.

Once inside, what had just happened started to hit me. My knees went wobbly, I started to shake and slumped down heavily on the sofa. DC Miller asked, "Why are you shaking?" with a sort of sneer in his voice. I tried to explain that I was in shock. "But I ain't done no murder," I insisted.

Sitting there in my lounge, with these two detectives waiting for the reinforcements they had called up, the full enormity slowly sank in. I felt completely helpless.

Within ten minutes I had my first meeting with DI Keith Pedder, and it wasn't very pleasant.

He was a big bloke in a smart suit who filled the room with his presence. He was very matter-of-fact as he asked me to confirm that I understood I'd been arrested on suspicion of murdering Rachel. I got the impression that he was putting on this casual 'just routine' air. Inside, I believe he was coiled up tight as a drum. Ready to spring out at me.

Next he gave me a form that he said was a warrant entitling him to search my home in connection with that offence. By now I was truly in a state of shock. Within a matter of minutes, what had started out as a routine day had seen my world turn upside down.

I was still shaking as Pedder reached down and picked up my copy of the *Daily Mirror*, lying unopened on my coffee table. He later claimed that it was open to page 19, which carried the *Crimewatch* appeal story and the Jane Harriman photofit. It wasn't true, but by then it wouldn't matter.

What *did* happen is that he turned to the photofit page and said, "Well Colin, that looks remarkably like you to me. What do you think?" There was a note of triumph in his voice.

I told him it was nothing like me. But he ignored it and went on. "Well, I think it looks extremely like you. Didn't you watch the TV last night?" When I confirmed that I had watched *Crimewatch*, he said, "So you can't be too surprised to see us here this morning?"

I told him there might be a vague resemblance, but they had said the suspect was over five foot ten and I'm only five foot seven – that's a big difference. I also pointed out that I didn't have a white button-up shirt and wouldn't be seen dead with one of those poofy little bum bags around my waist.

But they thought they could smell blood by then, in the shape of some wall-mounted decorations. As they would describe them, "fixed all around the room were a number of swords and large knives. Over the fireplace was a shield and crossed swords."

About this time, DCI Wickerson arrived with more police reinforcements and gave orders for the search to continue. They took me upstairs with them and what they found there got them very excited. On my bookshelves, according to them, "most of the titles were on the occult".

In my bedroom they were intrigued by my bedside 'altar', a couple of shelves with "various pictures and trinkets of the occult", as they saw it. Moving into the spare room, they were really licking their lips. It was all painted black, and on the threadbare carpet was an eight-inch wide pentagram star within a circle of white gloss paint. Small stones were positioned around the circle, with a triangular piece of grey painted wood in the centre. There were chalk drawings all over the wall of a horned god, and a very detailed painting of the Norse god Odin being tormented while tied to a tree.

Things got even better for them when they opened a cupboard and found my camping and survival gear – including a couple of big sheath knives. According to the police, the last item they pulled out was a black hooded cloak. This confirmed their view of me as a Satanist. It was also enough to daub me with the 'black magic' tag that still haunts me to this day, because they fed the story to the press, who lapped it up.

The truth, like so much of what happened in the Nickell murder inquiry, is very different if interpreted realistically.

I have a small collection of brass objects over my fireplace. They include some horse brasses, and two small, blunt-edged brass paper knives. (One is from HMS Belfast and the other is a tourist's souvenir of London.) When the police began their search there were also two brass plaques, one of an eagle and one of a stag. In addition there was a 1970s-style 'coat of arms' – a wall decoration with two blunt crossed swords welded to it. These were the only 'swords and large knives' in the room. Not exactly the Devil's armoury.

As for my books, only one – "a biography of the early twentieth-century self-styled Satanist Aleister Crowley", as one tabloid put it – had any link to the dark side of the occult. Two or three other books dealt with Wicca and other New Age beliefs, which I was interested in at the time, and I also had the famous author Colin Wilson's *Giant Book of the Supernatural*.

The rest of my library consisted of serious history books, mainly dealing with our Celtic, Saxon and early English rulers. I remember arguing with one of the coppers that the present royal family were only pretenders to the throne. When he said, "What about the Tudors?", I pointed out that the Windsors are a German family who only date from the beginning of the eighteenth century. They have no links to English history.

(A highly educated history graduate, who saw my library a few years later, told me that the majority of my books were reasonably heavyweight academic titles.)

My bedroom 'altar' consisted of two shelves my brother took from a church that was being demolished. They held some candles, two small black ornament bowls and a painting of the god Pan. With regard to the 'Black Room', as the police called it, there was nothing sinister or satanic about it. Shortly before I threw my brother Peter out, in 1986, he had become interested in heavy metal music and drugs. He painted the walls and ceiling black, painted a wooden crucifix red and hung it upside down on the wall above his bed. I painted the pentagram on the floor as part of my interest in the age-old religion of Wicca – which, in terms of occult belief, is far more to do with 'white magic'. It was just another aspect of the New Age cycle I was going through.

As for the 'black cowled cloak' that the police made so much of, it was, in fact, an olive-green, army surplus poncho! It's still there, in the same cupboard today.

The police's distortion of reality was to become fixed in the public's mind for the next fifteen years. Some of it I can laugh about now. At the time it was a bloody nightmare.

From that first morning they thought they had got their man. After completing their search of the flat they seized bagfuls of clothing and possessions, and carted the lot – and me – back to Wimbledon police station. Before leaving, I asked them to take my dog Brandy back to his former owner, who lived nearby, to look after until I was 'back later' that day. They must have thought I was naïve.

They had three days to bring a formal charge or release me. For DI Pedder, the profiler Paul Britton and the rest of the murder squad, I was now the prime suspect. They weren't going to let me go easily.

THREE

Despite all the shit that I've been through since that summer – the dodgy witnesses, the biased police, the press and public witch-hunts and personal betrayals – there's only one person that I have come to hate.

I blame him for all the bad things that have happened to me. He has even made bundles of cash out of my misfortunes. His initial invoice for 'assistance' on the Nickell murder investigation was billed at £300 an hour! The total was massive – "much reduced on audit," so Pedder would later claim – and he got a bestselling book out of me, and some other cases. But when his judgement of me was shown to be fatally flawed, he lacked the decency to even apologise.

That man is Paul Britton, and so far he's got away with assassinating my character.

Funnily enough, I watched him recently when he turned up as a talking head on a Channel 5 programme about the 'Real Dick Turpin'. It was one of those documentaries that hold about fifteen minutes of interesting facts and are then padded out to an hour with a load of psychobabble. Britton was in his element. Poor old Dick was a real eighteenth-century Essex Boy. A butcher turned housebreaker, then highwayman, who killed twice, he was finally hanged in York for horse stealing.

Sure enough, Britton had him neatly profiled – two hundred and seventy two years after his death, on very little evidence – as some sort of psychopath. I sympathised with the legendary rogue. I knew to my cost how lethal a Britton 'profile' could be. I had to hold myself from kicking the screen whenever his self-satisfied face appeared. My only comfort was that this was a comedown from the sort of heavyweight programmes he used to appear on. Perhaps his standing had nosedived as more and more people came to realise the flaws in his diagnoses.

At the time of Rachel's murder, Paul Britton was head of the Trent Regional Forensic Psychology Service in Leicester. Since 1983, he had assisted the police on a number of sex murder and rape cases in which he used psychological insights to build up profiles of the unidentified offenders. This led to him planning strategies for catching them, and, to be fair, he did have a spectacular success in his first big case.

This brought him more police work and, over the years, he perpetuated the myth that he was the inspiration for the Robbie Coltrane profiler in TV's *Cracker*, although he was only one of a number of pioneers. Later, helping police identify the killers of little Jamie Bulger, in 1993, and working on the 1994 Fred West/'House of Horrors' case would raise his profile even more.

Like a lot of arrogant people Britton was good at his job, but he came to believe that his conclusions and insights were like the word of God: unchallengeable. At that early stage in the development of offender profiling, there wasn't much of a scientific basis to go on. Britton based his assessments on his own clinical experiences with sexual deviants over two decades. His input was to have a profound effect on the Nickell case, and a devastating impact on my life.

Professor David Canter, the man who really pioneered profiling in this country, had described it as "More an art than a science," and added the following warning: "Profilers can get it seriously wrong." Prophetic, but unheeded, words.

By the end of July 1992, the Nickell investigation had reached an impasse. The police had trawled the records of known local sex offenders without result. They had dozens of witness statements but no match to the varied descriptions. And worst of all, they had recovered no forensic evidence from the crime scene – or at least, nothing that could be identified as such at the time.

Britton's arrival and subsequent analysis gave a new and worrying dimension to their investigation. It didn't take him long to come to the view that they were dealing with a violent sexual psychopath who, in his view, would inevitably strike again. That was not good news for a stalled murder inquiry team.

In a departure from his usual methods, he wrote the detectives an initial one-page analysis of what he believed were the killer's fantasies and motivations. This read:

After examination of the source material I am of the opinion that the offender has a sexually deviant-based personality disturbance, detailed characteristics of which would be extremely uncommon in the general population and would represent a very small sub-group within those men who suffer from general sexual deviation.

I would also expect the offender's sexual fantasies to contain at least some of the following elements:

1) Adult women . . .

2) The woman would be used as a sexual object for the gratification of the offender . . .

3) There would be little evidence of intimate relationship building . . .

4) There would be sadistic content. It would involve a knife or knives, physical control and verbal abuse . . .

5) The submission of the female participant . . .

6) It would involve anal and vaginal assault . . .

7) It would involve the female participant exhibiting fear . . .

8) I would expect the elements of sexual frenzy which would culminate in the killing of the female participant . . .

I should emphasise that I would expect his fantasies to include some of the above points but not necessarily all of them and there is no point to expect that his masturbatory fantasies would be confined solely to those points.

Over the next few weeks, as Britton absorbed more background details to the murder, he became increasingly confident about what drove the killer psychologically. He told the detectives the number of sexual psychopaths in the population was relatively small. Their basic sexual needs were very strong, while their self-esteem and confidence remained very low, or failed to develop at all.

In his view their early attempts to form sexual relationships would have failed, leaving them with feelings of rejection or ridicule. An even smaller number of them were left with deep resentments that they needed to take out on someone else. According to him, this group would develop fantasy worlds over which they had total imaginative control. Combined with their powerful sexual needs, these fantasies would lead eventually – and inevitably – to violence and murder.

It was a combination of anger, bitterness and resentment. In their ordinary lives they had little control or influence over others, so they developed an alternative zone where they were strong and powerful. Britton believed all their fantasies would come to be based on sexual control, the coercion of women in imaginary relationships.

Such a person would have an enormously powerful visual fantasy system that would, in effect, become a virtual reality. And it was a reality that would need to become ever more extreme to maintain the same level of sexual pleasure. So it was inevitable that the man who killed Rachel would murder another young woman in the future, because of his strong deviant urges and fantasies.

He expected Rachel's killer to be a stranger to her, aged between twenty and thirty. He would probably live within walking distance of the common and be totally familiar with its geography. He also suggested that the man would be single, in a low-paid job or unemployed, and live a solitary lifestyle, either at home with his parents or alone in a flat or bedsit.

In all probability he would have unusual interests or hobbies, and possibly be into bodybuilding or martial arts. It was doubtful that he could drive. He would have a history of failed or unsatisfactory relationships, if any. And he would be interested in some form of pornography.

There was a fifty/fifty chance that he would also have a previous history of offending, though not necessarily of so serious an offence as murder. The murder itself would have been rehearsed in his fantasies, in general terms. The specifics would have been determined by the time, place and circumstances.

For a few days after the killing he would have been excited or upset, but then returned to his normal behaviour. Poor social skills would make it difficult for him to relate to women in ordinary conversation and he might suffer from some form of sexual dysfunction, such as impotence or premature ejaculation.

Thankfully I don't have any problems in that department, but it was my bad luck that, in so many other respects, this profile appeared to fit me like a glove. I was a jobless loner who felt unhappy about his looks – particularly my crooked teeth and lack of height.

My interests included reading, history, art, all aspects of nature and the animal world, and the ancient religion of Wicca. That, by way of some books on the occult, would later be turned into a 'black magic obsession' by the headline-obsessed tabloids and the blinkered murder squad.

I was twenty-nine, unemployed, and lived in a flat on my own. But I had never been interested in martial arts – although as a teenager, around the time of the kung fu film craze, I had made some rice flails. And years later I did install home gym equipment, to build up my puny physique and keep myself fit.

My relationships, such as they were, had left me totally lacking in self-confidence with women. I had asked loads of girls to go out with me, but few of them had wanted to know. Although I was still a virgin, I continued to have a healthy interest in sex.

On account of all the profiling coincidences, the police took my boring background as ironclad proof that I was the killer. They swallowed Britton's murder profile hook, line and sinker, and believed that it fitted me perfectly.

Nobody bothered to stop and think that, just maybe, the personal characteristics that he described could also belong to an ordinary bloke who literally wouldn't hurt a fly. There must have been dozens, if not hundreds, of geeky blokes like me around the Wimbledon, Putney and Wandsworth areas alone.

But the police were so glad to have a prime suspect in their sights at last that they didn't properly analyse my responses. It was just my bad luck that public opinion – how I've come to hate those two bloody words! – insisted on a result. I would become the sacrifice to Paul Britton's ego and Keith Pedder's obsession with finding the killer.

Britton calls himself the 'Jigsaw Man' – "piecing together details of a murder to form a complete picture of the killer", like *Cracker* or Tony Hill from *Wire in the Blood*. But that's TV, where they never get it wrong. Out in the real world mistakes happen all the time. In my case, he was allowed to make me into a monster and the police encouraged him every inch of the way.

The morning of my initial arrest became a blur. Everything happened so fast. I went from heading off to the surgery to being banged up in a police cell in what seemed like the blink of an eye.

I was scared and confused. I kept thinking it was a bad dream and I would wake up soon. Of course, I didn't. I was in their custody and they didn't want to let me go.

Unknown to me at the time, there was a tactical phone discussion going on between Pedder and Britton over the best way to approach me. As it happened they didn't need any strategy, as I was only too willing to answer questions. What a fool!

They must have thought it was Christmas when I timidly accepted a duty solicitor as my brief. Graeme Woods was earnest but totally ineffectual. His inexperience allowed the police a virtual free hand in their interviews – something I only came to realise too late.

He allowed the interrogations to go ahead with almost no interruptions on my behalf. I just thought that the quicker I answered everything they asked me, the quicker I would be out of there. The solicitor didn't try to stem my verbal flood. He must have realised the police would put the worst interpretation on things that I considered completely innocent.

In the event, he didn't stand up for me. It was his advice that later got me labelled with the 'sex offender' tag that has dogged me ever since.

The interviews became incessant and exhausting. I can see now that their initial line of questioning was designed to lull me into feeling at ease. They chatted about me and my family and my lifestyle, such as it was. Very soon they knew almost every aspect of my life and past history, and did everything to use this information against me.

They said nothing about the murder, but they were very interested in my spiritual beliefs. I was asked to explain the pentagram and the drawings. I stressed that it had nothing to do with Satan, as they seemed to think, but that it was based on the old pagan religion of these islands and Northern Europe, long before Christianity.

The spiritual value of life is very precious, I told them. All life – animal, insect, tree and plant – has a spirit, even a breath of wind or rocks. The American Indians and aboriginal peoples understand this. They seemed very sceptical, but that was what I believed, and still do. Though I admitted I'd taken a knife when I'd gone backpacking, in the event that I had to kill and skin an animal such as a rabbit in a survival situation.

"But to tell the truth," I said, "I've never done it and I don't think I ever could." Of course, they then asked if I regularly carried knives and I explained that I never did. They wanted to know about the chalk drawings on the walls. I think they thought they were occult symbols, but I explained they were simply depictions of two famous ancient monuments: the Cerne Abbas Giant and the Uffington Horse.

With hindsight, I can see they were trying to label me as some sort of black magician, Satanist or religious nut. But I can't see that I'm any weirder than almost a billion Christians who believe a man survived crucifixion and came back from the dead. Or Scientologists who ignore evolution and believe we are descended from an intergalactic race that landed here a few thousand years ago.

Questions then started to jump between my personal philosophy and the murder. It shows how stupidly trusting I was when they asked me if I'd ever seen Rachel before. I said I thought I'd seen someone looking like her about two years earlier, pushing a little baby in a buggy, but I wasn't sure. I was trying to be helpful. I should have kept my mouth shut.

They tried to make me think it wasn't as long as two years ago, and that I had confused the time lapse. But I was certain. What I didn't know was that Rachel had only been going to Wimbledon Common for the past six months, so it couldn't possibly have been her that I saw.

The questioning went on throughout the day and into the early evening, with just a couple of short breaks for meals. They wanted to know if I had ever suffered from mental illness or depression – I told them I had been deeply unhappy when my father died and when my dog was put to sleep, but that was all.

Then they homed in on the times I'd walked up to the common on the morning of the murder, and whether I'd ever visited the scene in the following months. I repeated what I'd told the young copper, Pc Andrew Couch, who had stopped me at the underpass on my second visit. They wanted to know what time that was. I couldn't be sure – sometime between 11 and 11.30am. "I reckon the policeman wrote down the time he spoke to me when he took my address," I told them.

But he hadn't. Inexplicably his first statement put the time at nearer midday, and in a second statement a month later he made it between 12.30 and one o'clock. I also admitted that I'd come across what I thought was the murder scene the previous month, when I found some bunches of flowers beside a tree during a walk on the common.

The questions went on and on, and by the time they put me back in a cell that evening I was exhausted. There was no rest for the police, however. They had two new witnesses to interview, which wasn't good news for me. Both of them cast serious doubt on my description and timescale of events.

That daft old woman Lillian Avid's version of meeting me on the morning of the murder got them excited, even though she was in fantasyland. In her statement she told them: "Colin came rushing towards me. He appeared very agitated and sort of excited. He asked if I had heard about the murder on Wimbledon Common. I then said to him, 'Was she murdered then?'

"He replied, 'Yes, the woman with the little child. I often used to stand there on top of the hill and look down where it happened.'

"I thought to myself, 'How does he know where it happened?' Then he said to me, 'I must have missed it by ten minutes. It was on my normal route.'

"He was so excited that I said to him, 'Are you sure you didn't do it?' because of the way he was acting.

"Colin just grinned and replied, 'Nah.' But I felt very edgy at the way he was behaving. There was something very odd about him that day.

"He made me feel sick with the way he was talking. It made me think he'd done it, because he's never been like that before, the way he was talking to me that day," she told them.

"He looked as though he'd just bathed. He was fairly pink and his hair was wet. His hair was always tidy but he looked extra clean, very immaculate. His clothing looked new to me, all fresh like.

"I didn't really look at his face too much, it was his clothes I was looking at. I was shocked as they were so smart.

"I was so perturbed I went home and telephoned my daughter for advice. I felt ill and sick and worried because I am naturally a nervous person."

Her daughter advised her to phone her fears through to the police, which she did. Obviously they gave her low priority, because nobody visited to take a statement. But when she saw the *Crimewatch* photofit she was: "Sick to my stomach. Gutted. The image was a very good image of Colin Stagg. It was his head, his hair, the style of his hair and his face." She had been coming to check my address prior to calling the police, when she saw me being arrested.

So that was her evidence. Clean clothes made me a killer! It was complete nonsense. I could understand her thinking it was odd if I had usually looked like a tramp and had suddenly spruced up. But I was always clean and smartly dressed, as much as my limited wardrobe would allow. And there's no doubt I was excited – because, as far as I'd been concerned, a little girl had been murdered on the common, where I walked every day of my life.

At that time I hadn't known it was a young mum out with her son. I certainly didn't say anything about missing the murder by ten minutes, or looking down on where it happened. She just invented that from what she read or saw on TV afterwards. They must have come to realise this, because towards the end of the next day's interviews one of them admitted she was "a bit doolally".

But if what this crazy woman had said got them going, then what Susan Gale had to say convinced them I was definitely in the frame.

News of my arrest had gone round the estate like wildfire. Susan lived nearby – I had known her by sight for years – and when she heard about me being in custody she contacted the incident room.

Her evidence was emphatic. At 9.25, the time I was dropping off to sleep on my sofa, she insisted she saw me coming onto the common as she was leaving through the Putney Vale underpass with her two dogs. If this was true, it meant I had lied about the timing of my first walk and, most importantly, it would put me on the common at the time of the murder.

She insisted she could clearly remember passing me that day, over two months earlier, because her mother-in-law had stayed that night and was fretting about collecting her pension. For that reason it stuck in her memory. She also described me as wearing blue jeans and a white T-shirt, and told them she thought she'd seen me wearing a bum bag a couple of times before, but wasn't sure if I was wearing it on that day.

When the police triumphantly presented me with her evidence, I had a simple explanation. She had mixed up her dates. It was the wrong day she was describing. I told them I clearly recalled passing her a few days later. It stuck in my mind because her dogs were always a bit aggressive and, as I approached her, she bent down to take hold of them. Brandy wasn't on a lead at the time, so I veered away from her, raising my hand as a 'hello' and a 'thank you' as I passed.

They obviously weren't convinced, but I stuck to my story. The only thing I was a bit vague about was the time I woke up after getting back from my first walk, and going out again to meet the policeman at the underpass.

It went on all day, Pedder and DC Martin Long taking it in turns to try to break my story. They suggested I was the bloke seen by some witnesses on the common carrying a black bag. I kept telling them I had never owned a bum bag or a holdall. It was ridiculous! I wouldn't be seen dead with one of those things round my waist. The only similar thing I have ever owned was a little red rucksack.

What they wanted was a confession, but that wasn't an option. "Everything I've told you is the exact truth. I'm not a murderer. I could never hit a woman even if I wanted to. I don't even hit my dog," I said.

It didn't make any difference. I could see they were convinced I was lying about the times I went over the common. And if I was lying about that, what else was I hiding? That was the extent of their argument.

By the Saturday night, a day and a half after my arrest, I was exhausted and scared. The questioning was relentless and they weren't interested in listening to my side of the story. I think they had made up their minds that I was the killer.

Then they came to take me to court to get an extension for further detention. They wanted to put a blanket over my head because the press were virtually camped outside the station, up ladders and in gardens, trying to get a picture of me. My solicitor agreed. He told me it was in my best interest, as otherwise it might adversely affect the identification parade to be held the next day. "You don't want any unnecessary publicity, and of course you might be innocent."

Thanks for the vote of confidence, Mr Woods, I thought.

The next morning I was driven to Brixton police station in handcuffs. I was taken to a large portacabin at the back of the building. There I met my solicitor and a 'responsible adult' from social services, a Mr Paul Bridge. I remember thinking to myself that I may have had a boyish face, but I wasn't so young that I needed adult supervision.

Then they explained the line-up procedure. I was led into a harshly lit room with a crowd of people and invited to dismiss those I didn't think resembled me. That was when I started to believe I wasn't going to get out of this mess, because none of the twenty-six men present looked like me.

I had close-cropped hair at the time and most of the others had long or medium-length hair. Neither did they facially resemble me very much. With the help of my solicitor, I indicated those who really looked nothing like me at all. But my heart wasn't in it. I felt the police had stacked the odds against me.

There were ten of us altogether, and we had to stand under these harsh white spotlights while five witnesses came to inspect us. Afterwards, I was told that only one person – it turned out to be Jane Harriman – had positively identified me as the man she saw shortly before the murder.

But her two eldest boys, who had also seen the man on three occasions with her, failed to pick me out. Nor did Amanda Phelan, who had watched a suspect washing his hands in the drainage ditch beside the murder scene.

Back in my cell, I was feeling very down. It didn't help when DC Lyle appeared at the door and said, "It's not looking good for you. Perhaps you should stop wasting time and just confess."

I snarled back at him, "It's looking very good for me because I'm not the fucking murderer!"

A little while later, another detective turned up. "Why don't you just tell us it was you?" he asked. "Because it wasn't!" I replied.

"Come on, we know it was you. It'll go easy on you if you tell us." I ignored him and asked after my dog, who was being kept in the station's kennels.

Over the next two days the pressure was relentless. They went over the same ground again and again until my head ached. They were being primed by Paul Britton via regular phone chats with DI Pedder, at every stage of their questioning. He told them to be calm but firm and make me realise that "the truth will inevitably come out."

They kept going over my family background, my beliefs, and what I did on the morning of the murder. Britton had advised them that any denials were evidence of my "basic cunning and intelligence". He didn't seem to consider that it could be the plain truth. Neither did Pedder, who was convinced I was lying. As far as I could see, the only 'truth' they wanted was my confession to killing Rachel Nickell.

Part of Britton's tactics was to get them to show me a horrific photo of Rachel's body at the scene. It was taken from behind her corpse at a distance of about fifteen to twenty feet. You couldn't see the stab wounds from that angle. Her naked buttocks were visible, with her trousers round her ankles. It was a cruel, undignified way to treat a human body.

This was designed to shock me, via the enormity of what I'd supposedly done, into confessing. Instead, I was just full of rage towards the bastard who did this to an innocent young mum.

In the course of this lengthy interrogation, I mentioned my enjoyment of nude sunbathing on remote parts of the common. They seized on it and made it into some sort of unhealthy fetish. I tried to explain I only did it in an area that had been used by hundreds of nude sunbathers for years. It wasn't officially recognised as such, but the common rangers turned a blind eye. So did regular common walkers.

There was nothing sinister or dirty involved. It was only about getting an all-over tan, but it gave them something concrete to go after me for. Trawling through reports of suspicious behaviour on the common some weeks after the murder, they found one from a woman who had complained about a nude sunbather 'exposing himself' to her.

She couldn't identify him, except to say that he had a large erection and he smiled at her. Like a fool, I said I remembered a woman disturbing me while I was sunbathing naked. I stressed that I hadn't been erect, and had tried to cover my penis by raising one leg as she passed. What followed was so unnecessary.

All I had to say to them was that I was mistaken about the date – "It wasn't me," or, "Hold an identity parade if you dare" – and it would never have got to court. Unfortunately, my stupid solicitor advised me to plead guilty and "get the case out of the way".

I even explained to him that I have a very high body temperature that makes clothing uncomfortable in hot weather.

That's why I liked sunbathing nude. It's also the reason I invariably wear cut-off T-shirts and no jacket in all but the coldest weather. (All my life, people have said to me in winter, "Aren't you cold?")

He took no notice and, because I wanted to get back to my home and my dog, I went along with him. It was the stupidest thing I've ever done in my life. My only excuse is that I was tired and frightened.

But it was a bonus for the Old Bill. They were on the point of having to let me go, because their 'evidence' against me was at best circumstantial and patchy. It was nowhere near solid enough for the Crown Prosecution Service to even think of mounting a case.

In fact, as I would discover years later, after Wickerson had retired to the Virgin Islands, the CPS had sent him, Bassett and Pedder a memo: "Not advisable to charge Stagg. It has little chance of success."

That was no surprise, considering what little they had against me. There was no forensic evidence, no witness (save for little Alex), no murder weapon, and only flimsy allegations and inferences against me that would have been torn to shreds by any defence counsel.

Now suddenly they could repay me for resisting them. It was to set a pattern for the years of payback to come from the police. They formally released me on police bail for the Rachel inquiry – with the proviso that I reported to them regularly – then gleefully charged me for the sunbathing incident and detained me overnight.

Being fined for indecent exposure still haunts me to this day. Being branded a flasher, a sex offender, would confirm the public's opinion that I was a dangerous deviant who got away with murder. In some respects, that minor conviction – for which I was fined £200 – blighted my life as much as the murder charge. I was badly let down when I most needed help, and so I sacked my solicitor.

The damage was done, but at least I was a free man again. All I wanted was to be reunited with my dog and left alone to get on with my quiet, humdrum life. My ordeal was over, so it seemed to me then.

If I'd known that little Alex had seemingly implicated another suspect, one month earlier, I would have felt even more confident.

After weeks of gentle questioning, the child had told his father he was afraid of a man named Andy Abrahams, who lived close to them and, for the six months prior to her death, had taken his son to school with Alex and Rachel.

And he had regularly visited Wimbledon Common with her and their two children. On the day of the murder, he had phoned the police to say he recognised his friend's Volvo being towed out of the Windmill car park.

After going in to give a statement he volunteered to identify her body, which detectives had thought was very strange behaviour. Other than being jobless, he did not fit the Britton profile in any way. He was strongly alibied – by his wife – as being in bed on the morning of the murder. But Alex's remarks made them look at him very closely.

The child gave similar answers when his father repeated the questions in front of a detective. Andre said, "Alex, do you want to see Andy?"

Alex replied, "No."

"Does Andy look like the man who hurt Mummy?"

"Yes."

"Do you think he is the man who hurt Mummy?"

"Yes."

"Was it Andy?"

"Yes."

This was obviously very worrying. Although Alex's testimony was dubious as evidence, it raised questions about Abrahams. The detectives remembered taking him to the common to demonstrate where he and Rachel walked with their boys and their dogs. Alex had been there too, and became visibly distressed at the sight of Andy.

They were also surprised that, according to his story, he had not taken his two dogs out for exercise since the previous evening. If Abrahams was to be believed, it meant they had been locked in his first-floor flat with no garden access and nowhere to go to the toilet.

It was decided that he needed much closer scrutiny. Pedder came up with the bright idea of taking the couple in for questioning while bugging their flat. This scheme was eventually turned down, but it was agreed to set up a secret observation to test how accurately he'd described his daily routine.

After six weeks it was agreed that Abrahams was a lazy slob who stayed in bed far too long, but his habits were not at odds with his alibi statement. Still, they decided there was enough weight in Alex's words to bring him in and put him under the Wickerson/Pedder grill. He came out toasted but still protesting his innocence. He had also admitted being besotted by Rachel, telling them, "I did fancy her, but because you fancy someone sexually doesn't mean that you have to go and make a do of it.

"I didn't try anything on with her. I didn't make a pass at her. She was a very, very nice person. I was glad to be seen out with her."

But he was unable to explain why Rachel had blanked him for over a week prior to her death. Wickerson suggested he had made a clumsy pass at her and had been rejected. This humiliation had led him to follow her to the common and kill her in revenge. Abrahams, in floods of tears, repeatedly denied the accusation.

A search of his flat revealed faded bloodstains on his trainers. He claimed a garage door had come down on his head, months earlier, and efforts to identify the origin of the tiny spatters were unsuccessful.

I discovered later that Abrahams, who was twenty-seven, bore a resemblance to me, and therefore also to the *Crimewatch* photofit. Yet he was never put in a line-up before Jane Harriman; nor did they consider showing video footage of *me* to Alex.

They had a suspect who had known the deceased for six months; he was besotted with her; he may have been rejected by her, and his only alibi was his wife – who, he admitted in his statement, would lie for him!

For years afterwards I still regarded him with a lot of suspicion. But in 2000 a cold-case review, using advanced new DNA techniques, would re-examine the tiny blood splatters on his trainers and fail to match them to Rachel.

Of course, he never matched Britton's profile of the killer either – unlike me. It's always puzzled me why Britton's advice was never sought during his series of interviews. If only on the face of it, this man had seemed to make for a much more compelling prime suspect.

It's equally strange that Britton subsequently tried to disguise his hands-on involvement in my initial questioning. His autobiography, written three years after the case collapsed and his role was savaged by the judge, denies any knowledge of me until after my release on September 21st 1992.

In *The Jigsaw Man*, he writes about a phone call from John Basseett in late September. One of his officers had a request to make, he said, and then he introduced Detective Inspector Keith Pedder.

"Pedder chose his words carefully. 'I've spent about fourteen hours interviewing a man we have reason to believe might be able to help us in connection with the Nickell murder . . .

"'What I need to know is if there is anything in the interviews that would allow you to say categorically that, in your opinion, this man could not be responsible for the murder of Rachel Nickell, based upon the offender profile and deviant sexuality analysis that you gave us.'"

It appears he has never had previous contact with Pedder and is being asked to analyse tapes made some time earlier. But Pedder's version of events is very different: "Before starting the interviews I therefore rang Paul Britton at the Tower Hotel in Leicester and asked if he would want to give any specific advice as to how I should approach him."

If that wasn't clear enough, Pedder insists, "Throughout the interviews, as and when Mr Stagg's behaviour appeared to be contradictory, I would ring Paul Britton. According to him, Stagg's denials were indicative of his cunning and basic intelligence."

He is adamant that Britton was involved from the very outset and helped in setting the framework of my interrogation. This gaping discrepancy could, perhaps, be explained by Britton's desire to play down his pivotal role in building the case against me, which backfired so badly. If so, he failed miserably.

From what he says about my 'cunning', it's clear his perception of me was already coloured in shades of black. But he had a lot worse in store for me, as I was to find out later.

FOUR

Running out of Wimbledon Magistrates' Court, I was immediately mobbed by a press scrum. The TV lights were blinding as dozens of reporters and cameramen jostled, fighting for pictures and bellowing questions.

It was madness. All I could think of was getting back to the police station, picking up Brandy and going home. I barged through the press pack, knocking over some camera gear, and legged it, with the vultures in pursuit.

At the station I had to wait well over an hour for them to bring Brandy out to me. It was another petty act of revenge for defying them. So was making me find my own way home. I had no money and I was about three miles from Roehampton. I had never been into Wimbledon town centre before and I got lost several times, before I reached the common and familiar surroundings.

A photographer ambushed me on the way, but by the time I reached my front door the media had disappeared and I naïvely thought my ordeal was over. In fact it was only just beginning.

I got my first taste of what life was going to be like when I walked down to my local shops the next morning. Passing two women who were talking about me, I heard one of them say, "That's him, the pervert!" I soon discovered that my face and address had been plastered across most of the newspapers and TV. In the shops, some customers pointedly turned away from me, muttering.

Later that day, some kids shouted "nonce!" at me for the first time. It made me feel sick, but I was determined to put a brave face on it. From thereon, almost every time I went out, both teenagers and adults would call me names: killer, sicko, bastard, pervert, nonce were the usual terms of abuse.

Some close neighbours were supportive, but I was cold-shouldered by a lot of people I had known to say 'hello' to for years. That was very hurtful, but I hoped that, if I showed people I'd done nothing to be ashamed of, things would return to normal. It was a forlorn hope.

Meanwhile, the police were still twisting the knife. They refused to return all the clothes and possessions they had removed from my flat, their excuse being that forensic analysis took a long time. I was left with almost nothing to wear, except the clothes I stood up in. It took five months and a new solicitor to get everything back. But by then the sickening pattern of my new life had been set in stone.

The level of hatred towards me was both astonishing and frightening. I couldn't have imagined the way that people – often complete strangers – would turn on me. It caught me completely unprepared. I had lived on the Alton estate most of my life, without having a serious cross word with anyone. I was always polite to people and, if I didn't frequent the local pubs or have lots of friends, by the same token I didn't have any enemies that I knew about.

All that changed after my release. Over the next six months, I came to feel that almost everybody's hand was turned against me. I was a marked man. For the first time in my life I started to develop a siege mentality. My home became my castle where I pulled up the drawbridge, the only sanctuary where I could hide – although not always in safety.

It became a local 'sport' for drinkers returning from the pubs to run along our balcony and hammer my front door or bang on the windows. They would also kick my back gate and chuck stones into the garden. Eggs were thrown at my windows, or sometimes at me when I was out with the dog.

One teenage druggie in particular was always harassing me. Sometimes he would be on his own, other times with some of the local tearaways. He was responsible for when my window was broken for the first time. I reported him to the police, because I needed a crime number for the council's insurance purposes, but they said they couldn't prove it was him, and did nothing.

Over the following months I made numerous complaints, about intimidation and attacks on my home, to both Wandsworth and Putney police stations, which were largely ignored. The police disinterest told me clearly that I could never expect their assistance while the abuse continued.

Initially I hoped interest in me would gradually die down. I naïvely thought the press and the police would find another scapegoat, or just forget about me. But it went on, and I withdrew more and more into myself. I had lost my newspaper round after many years. (The newsagent's excuse was that he found someone else while I was in police custody.) People in shops would turn their backs on me. Some shop assistants would deliberately ignore me, in the hope that I'd get the message and go away. Passers-by continued to call me names or scowl at me.

A couple of times I was threatened, and then the hate mail

started. I couldn't get my head round some of the vicious things they said about me, but a lot of it was down to the newspapers, who had declared open season on me – aided and abetted by the police. There were stories about my 'black magic' practices and devil worship. Coupled with being prime suspect in the Nickell case – something the police always managed to hint at without coming right out and saying it – plus the nude sunbathing conviction, I was deemed fair game.

Typical of the nonsense and downright lies printed about me was a big story by a girl reporter from one of the tabloids. She claimed to have interviewed me in my 'voodoo lair'. She wrote a big story about how she had sat in my weird living room, surrounded by creepy occult symbols. Apparently she was made very uneasy by the way I kept staring at her, after I had served her coffee in a chipped and dirty mug. She "trembled with fear" as I stared out fixedly at her. Afterwards, she wrote that a senior police officer had warned her to "never go into that place alone again".

The truth was very different. She never got into the house – I never let any strangers in. I think I may have spoken briefly through a crack in the door before closing it firmly in her face, and that was all. The only pictures the paper took were of my front door. And the reporter could only have got the Wicca symbols angle from the police. They were in an upstairs bedroom and there was nothing in my living room. The police had taken all the brasses away and not yet returned them.

She made the whole thing up. But people believed it. There were lots of stories like this, I suspect helped by tips and off-the-record briefings by the police to keep the pressure on me. It spelled out quite clearly that they still considered me a dangerous prime suspect, and were prepared to fuel the public's prejudices against me.

According to the mentality of local people, women were not

safe near me. I was often called a murderer, and one letter writer described me as a 'lady killer'. I was always considered a bit odd because I was a loner who kept to myself, so it didn't take long to become a local hate figure.

Although I tried to put a brave face on things, I was starting to feel intimidated whenever I went out. It made me change my daily routine. I started to take my dog for very early morning walks – something I still do – when very few people were about. It felt safer that way.

(Even recently, I was accosted while walking my dogs in Richmond Park where I always go now. "You're that bloke that murdered Rachel Nickell, aren't you?" said some other bloke I'd never met. I reported the incident to the park ranger, but he said sorry, there was nothing he could do.)

At the time of my first release from custody I still went over to Wimbledon Common, because I couldn't drive and it was the closest place to exercise my dog. I suppose we must have passed the murder site lots of times, but I never knew exactly where it was. The place where flowers had been left was apparently some distance away.

So my life moved into a new, unsettling period where I was always on my guard. I lost the self-assurance I had always enjoyed (except with women), and became even more reclusive and introspective.

I did, however, manage to find some solace with a local woman, Susanne, who I'd known all my life. It wasn't a proper affair, but she helped make things bearable. She was female company, and enjoying heavy petting with her made me feel better about myself.

I kept telling myself I would 'get laid' one of these days, and in the meantime I travelled in hope of passing my virginity milestone. It was this obsession that had led me to reply to a lonely hearts ad in the personal columns of *Loot,* about eighteen months before Rachel's murder. It was another naïve search for sex that would backfire badly, confirming me in the police's view as their prime suspect.

The ad read: *Lonely, shy overweight, white woman, age 33, not very attractive, separated and waiting divorce, looking for white guy, 28-38, who like myself is understanding, loving, likes home life. Must be non-smoker and love animals. Is this you, why not write now? Box 6109.*

I responded in kind. Her name was Julie Pines and, to be honest, I didn't care what she looked like. After all, to me she was a sexually experienced woman. She sounded nice, and she might be grateful enough for my interest to give me a shag!

We exchanged quite a few letters, detailing our interests and hobbies and that sort of stuff, and spoke regularly on the phone. Then, stupidly, I thought I would spice things up a bit by suggesting we send each other details of our secret fantasies. It was a clumsy way to introduce the possibility of sex into our relationship.

I was, in effect, testing the water. At that stage of my life I wasn't as articulate as I am now, so I was far more comfortable with writing than speaking. I stressed I was not a weirdo or a pervert, but I had never before had anyone to confide in about my sexual dreams and thought it might be a turn-on. I also assured her I would understand if she wasn't keen on the idea

Julie didn't say no, so I went ahead. I enjoy writing and I described a very straight but sexy scenario that I hoped would excite her. The setting was outdoors in a park on a beautiful summer day. I am sunbathing naked and gently masturbating when a woman approaches. Instead of being shocked and disgusted she is turned on, strips off and invites me to have sex with her. That's the full extent of it. No perversion. No sadism. No violence. Just what I can see now as a simple adolescent fantasy.

By today's standards, and even the reader's letters in the adult magazines of the day, it was very tame. Or so I thought.

I got a furious reply saying it was 'filthy' and 'disgusting', and she never wanted to hear from me again. She never did, but the police certainly heard from her after I had first been arrested.

She saw me on TV, running away from court after my release from police custody. She recognised my name and immediately phoned them about the man who had so upset her with his steamy fantasy letter. I learnt later that, despite telling me she was 'shocked and disgusted' by my note, which she'd immediately thrown in the dustbin, she had in fact kept it.

I could never get my head round why she did that. It was very odd behaviour for someone who professed to be so outraged.

Whatever her reasons, it was bad news for me. But Julie's call to the murder squad couldn't have come at a better time for them. After being forced to let me go, their inquiry had run out of steam. They had exhausted all leads, and senior officers at the Yard were talking of scaling back resources and redeploying some of the manpower.

At this low point, Julie Pines' call seemed to justify their already blinkered suspicions of me, and forced the investigation down an entirely new path. DI Pedder was intrigued by the possibilities for a 'sting' that my fantasy letter to Julie seemed to open up for him.

He contacted SO10, the crack undercover operations unit, to check the feasibility of setting me up with a view to extracting a confession. They gave his idea the go-ahead in principle, subject to input from Paul Britton. Pedder was delighted.

From then on the plan developed a momentum of its own. Within days of my release, the team leaders – Bassett, Wickerson and Pedder – travelled to Leicester for a fateful conference with the 'Jigsaw Man'.

I had a chance to learn later what happened at that crucial

meeting from my legal team. The murder squad wanted to know if it was possible to design a special undercover operation, based on his analysis of the killer's deviant sexuality. One that would either eliminate or implicate their prime suspect.

Britton was intrigued by the psychological challenge. He claimed that, if the killer built up a relationship with someone, he might feel safe enough to reveal his involvement to them. But he warned that the plan would involve someone, preferably a policewoman, getting close to the subject over a period of time.

The aim was to create a sort of intimacy whereby their suspect would eventually choose to disclose aspects of his 'sexual functioning'. According to Britton, their target would face a lot of critical decision points along the way. It would be his choice alone which direction he took. The operation would only continue if the suspect chose a "previously specified and very particular pathway" each time. Any deviation from this specific route would eliminate him.

As Britton put it, "It will require your suspect to actively climb a series of ladders. He either eliminates or implicates himself by his own choices." He stressed it would not be the equivalent of putting someone on the top of a slide and giving him a push. It would always be down to the suspect as to which way he went.

This seemingly ethical approach was endorsed by Pedder. As he put it, "Nobody wants the wrong person charged and the real killer left out there to kill again." Those words would come back to haunt him – as they would me. As would the 'ethical operation' bullshit. For I wasn't just to be given a gentle nudge, I would be very forcefully shoved!

The murder team were delighted and excited by Britton's scheme. At last they had something practical to work with. It seemed to offer a kick-start to the stalled inquiry. They agreed to make initial contact by letter, using Julie Pines as a point of reference.

Britton was convinced that, with the right confidante, the killer would reveal fantasies that would clearly show a need for "extremely violent non-consensual sexual activity".

Pedder wanted to know whether he would be able to say for certain that the suspect was also the killer, should the results match Britton's detailed profile. He told the three officers that such a match would only show the suspect and the killer shared the same extremely rare "sexually deviant-based personality disorder".

But the chances of two such persons being on the common at the same time were, in his words, "vanishingly small". That removed any lingering doubts.

Now it only needed the blessing of the Yard's top brass and, of course, the Crown Prosecution Service. There would have been no point in going ahead if it was likely to be ruled unethical or inadmissible in court.

To Pedder's delight the CPS gave it the legal green light. So a mission statement, outlining the nuts and bolts of the operation, was sent up the police chain of command. It passed through the hands of half a dozen senior Met officers – all of whom were enthusiastic – before being given the final go-ahead by no less a personage than the Assistant Deputy Commissioner, Ian Johnston.

So that's how the murder inquiry, queerly named Operation Edzell, spawned a bastard son – Edzell 2, directed solely against me. According to Britton, a 'designer friendship' that they created would inevitably lead to proof of my guilt or innocence. No leeway for doubt, or allowances for someone with a slightly different temperament. I'm also sure that he suggested a woman because he knew she would promise me a shag, and that with that sort of incentive I might say anything just to 'get a result'.

In the months after my release I learned for the first time in my life what it really means to be hated by complete strangers.

Nothing prepares you for that feeling of being an outcast. I suppose people feel a lot better about themselves – however rotten they are – if they have someone to look down on. I'm sure that's why some of my worst tormentors were local drug dealers, addicts and petty criminals, who could stand on a moral molehill for the first time in their lives.

But as the months passed, the levels of malice started to drop off. (Though there was some nasty hate mail and one bloke threatened to punch me, but backed off when I stood my ground.) I began to hope that public opinion had changed, or that at least they had forgotten about me. The police certainly seemed to have lost interest.

In January they cancelled my bail requirements and returned most of my property. I was no longer on their radar – so I thought. But they were deliberately downplaying their interest in me to allay any suspicions of what was to come.

That was when Lizzie James sneaked into my life.

I had genuinely forgotten about Julie Pines. It had been nearly two years since we had been in touch, and for someone to contact me out of the blue, using her as an introduction, should have seemed suspicious. But back then I was a lot less savvy and took everything at face value. My name and address had appeared in all the papers, and for a couple of months after my release a woman from Wales had written to me.

So Lizzie's first letter wasn't that much of a surprise, even if her link with Julie was. Truth be told, I was flattered by her interest in me – which is exactly what she wanted. It was deception on a very basic level, and I fell for it.

FIVE

When Operation Edzell kicked off, on January 19th 1993, I was blissfully unaware of its existence. It began with the arrival of a letter from the woman claiming to be my secret admirer.

According to Lizzie James, she had read my raunchy letter that so disgusted Julie Pines, and it had turned her on. I have to admit I was too flattered and excited to question her motives. Her letter read:

Dear Colin,

I hope you are not offended by this intrusion as we have never met before, but I feel that I have known you for years.

You may remember writing to a woman called Julie. Julie was an old friend of mine and a little old fashioned in her outlook (if you know what I mean!) A while ago when I stayed with her, while she was out I read a letter that you had sent her (I hope you remember).

This letter has been on my mind and interests me greatly, I find myself thinking of you a lot. I would be very interested in getting to know you more and writing to you again. I will tell you a little about myself. I am divorced (like Julie) and quite frankly have had my fill of shallow, one way relationships, as I have had my fingers burnt too many times.

I am five foot eight, blonde, aged thirty and I have been called attractive in the past. My interests may sound boring, but I don't socialise much and prefer my own company.

I read a lot and often contemplated writing a book. I have an odd taste in music, my favourite record being 'Walk on the Wild Side' by Lou Reed. I am a bit cautious but not paranoid, I would appreciate it if you didn't let Julie know that I've written to you as our friendship has dwindled.

I have taken an accommodation address in London so you can contact me there. (I am in the process of moving flats and I don't want any letters going missing).

I am in central London about twice a week. I hope you are not upset by this letter and look forward to hearing from you soon.

Lizzie X

P.S. My name is Lizzie James.

Reading these words now, it's quite clear that she was referring to my sexual fantasy letter and was giving the impression she had been turned on by it. She wanted more of the same, or even more so.

There's no other interpretation. It shows that the whole fantasy sex scenario was instigated by her from the outset – or, rather, by Britton. And I happily went along with the idea, just as he had hoped.

It had taken four months of high-level talks between senior police officers, CPS lawyers and the murder squad to work out the mechanics of this operation. Britton was to provide the guidelines for each letter, directing what it should contain and what it should reflect. The police were to find the words and syntax. My responses would be analysed by Britton who would then plot their next move.

Keith Pedder was completely sold on the idea and was dead keen to get it up and running. He took the view that, although Britton would never be able to say categorically that I was the killer without a confession, or hard evidence like the murder knife, it would be enough to go to a jury.

That was what he desperately wanted, because he believed — and I think he was correct — that a jury could have been persuaded that I was the killer. They would, like Britton, think that the chances of two people sharing this form of sexual deviance and being on Wimbledon Common at the same time were "vanishingly small".

Pedder guessed that the twelve good people and true would hear Britton's evidence, my letters to Lizzie and the police allegation that I had lied about my times on the common, and then find me guilty — because, taken together, it all seemed too compelling not to be true. I would have been sent down for life. It could so easily have happened. It so nearly did.

To their apparent surprise, I responded to Lizzie's initial letter within days. At the time I couldn't remember exactly what I had written to Julie, so I asked Lizzie to remind me. I also gave her a lot of bog-standard personal details about myself, asking her to do the same and send me her photograph. My prompt response seems to have got them drooling, because in it I had also written:

We must each find our own paths to travel along. I do not like people who are closed minded.

I'll admit to you that every summer I like to do a bit of nude sunbathing over my local park, in a secluded spot of course, just to get an all-over tan. But people think that is 'perverted'. Small minds, small intelligence.

And I hinted that I would like to get to know her more 'intimately'.

Her response, on January 27th, began:

Thank you for writing back. At first I was a bit worried about posting my letter to you, but when I saw your reply I was pleased and reassured, even though you've only written back once I don't feel as if we're strangers.

It's nice to know that there is a like mind out there, sometimes I get lonely (like you) and find it difficult to get on with other women, but then I find them so boring and trivial, I don't want to know them!

She went on in a way that definitely suggested she was up for sex.

I sometimes long for company, (only the kind that a man can give.) My ex-friend and your ex-penfriend was a boring old bag, prudish.

She didn't really know how to enjoy herself. I hope you can remember, you wrote to her about your feelings and personal thoughts.

The letter I read was very revealing, in more ways than one and I think we both have a lot in common. I noticed your taste in books is a bit different to mine. I prefer generally heavy-going plots with twisted endings.

I've just finished reading a really good book. It's about how passion turns bitter and has a real tragic ending.

All this sounded even more encouraging to me. By then I'd remembered writing an explicit fantasy letter to a woman called Julie some years before. I wrote back and told Lizzie as much, adding:

That letter was a bit explicit. I can, if you want, enclose a 'personal' letter with this one, about a fantasy I have had since you first wrote to me.

You have been on my mind ever since. I hope you are not offended by my 'letters'. It's just I have always had an open mind about sex, but I've never really found anyone on the same wavelength. I bet you've had a few fantasies yourself.

In fact I did enclose this fantasy, because in her opening letter she seemed to be excited by the one I wrote to Julie. It included mutual masturbation in the back garden and 'hot' sex in a variety of positions, in my bedroom throughout the night. I wrote:

Luckily all the neighbours are in bed, so no-one can see us, but the thought that someone might, excites us both.

You lay on the warm damp grass holding my hand. I sit astride you slowly masturbating myself, as I stroke your hair, you're laying there smiling.

However, to show I was also interested in her as a person and not simply as a sex object, I added:

I would like it very much if I could send you letters like this about my fantasies, about us being together.

It would make me happy if you did the same, telling me about your feelings and fantasies and what you would like to do when we get together, (if you know what I mean!)

After that, we swapped Valentine cards and I awaited her next letter with anticipation. I was happy and excited. I couldn't believe how my luck had changed. It almost seemed too good to be true. And it was – but I wasn't to know what was going on behind the scenes.

Britton is said to have found my fantasy line 'unexceptional', much to the police's disappointment. He viewed it as normal 'porn mag fodder' with a preference for outdoor sex. (Of course, he ignored my love of nature and the outdoors in general, which should have been clear from my hours of police interviews.)

I wrote to Lizzie again a few days later:

I hope my last letter to you was okay and I hope my photograph didn't frighten you. I can't wait to see your photograph so that I can put a face to your letters.

I bet you're a very sexy, gorgeous woman. I hope we will have a great exciting relationship together, that will last for a very long time.

I also invited her to visit. But I advised her:

If you are a bit wary then bring a friend, for I know that there are lots of dangers for women (and children) these days with all these weirdos and nutters about.

Encouraged by her apparent interest in sexual fantasy, I included another scene involving both of us indulging in oral sex and intercourse, which I tried to make more romantic. I also added:

I can't wait to see you Lizzie. Every day I think about you, wondering more about you, longing to hold you near to me, feeling your warm vibrant body close to mine, pressing my lips close to yours, taking your passionate heart for myself.

Lizzie wrote back, enclosing a photo. She looked stunning with her long blonde hair and beautiful face. I couldn't believe my luck.

(What I didn't know was that she had been 'doctored' for the photo. Expensive hair extensions and a coy look back over her shoulder meant that half her face was hidden. Her own mother wouldn't have known her from that snapshot.)

Her letter was even more encouraging. She wrote:

Your letters were certainly very enlightening and I did enjoy reading them, the first one was so real, if I closed my eyes I could almost feel you, sat astride me and feel your weight pressing me into the grass.

Your second letter I viewed as an extra treat. You really write well and I bet this is just the tip of the iceberg when it comes to your thoughts.

There's a lot more to you than meets the eye, Colin. I'm sure your fantasies hold no bounds and you are as broad minded and uninhibited as me, I can't wait for your next letter, you have a clever mind and you're a brilliant 'story teller', you'll have to wait for a letter like that from me, (I'm a little slow to start, but I'm working myself up for the big one.) (Ha! Ha!)

She ended up by saying:

Write soon Colin, I can't wait to get your letter in my 'little handies'.
Love. Lizzie x.

That seemed to make it crystal clear – or at least as clear as Britton had intended – that she was 'well up' for more sexy stories. I replied by return of post. My letter was in two parts. Initially I tried to build on our relationship by telling her a lot more about my personal background, family life and beliefs. I also let my feelings show:

Thank you for your letter and that beautiful photograph. I couldn't believe how attractive and sexy you look. You are very beautiful Lizzie with that lovely long hair and those sexy eyes.

I'm so glad that you liked my 'letters' and that you too are as broad-minded and uninhibited as me, I can't wait to read some of your fantasies!

Under the heading 'A Special Treat for My Beautiful Lizzie', I also enclosed another steamily romantic (or so I thought) sex story.

Once more I chose an outdoor, woodland location, in a small clearing by a fallen tree and a stream, where we chill our picnic lunch wine. We undress and I lead her to a fallen tree, bending her over the trunk so I can have her from behind. She gives a stifled moan and I immediately ask if she's all right. "Yes, that's wonderful," she moans. (I mention this to show that, even in fantasy role-play, I was concerned not to hurt my partner.)

After some more graphic descriptions of front- and back-entry sex sessions, we are holding each other tenderly:

I raise myself off you and press my lips to yours, making you open your eyes. A few tear drops run down your cheeks as you say "I love you so much."

I reply "You look so beautiful laying here, let's never be separated. You're the only woman I will ever want. You're delicious, so full, so hot and vibrant. I love you Lizzie."

Looking back, fourteen years later, I'm embarrassed by myself. It's schoolboy stuff, adolescent fantasy followed by a big dollop of Mills and Boon sugar. But it really got Pedder going. Apparently, he rushed around the squad room shouting, "Look, he's there, he's in the woods. It's just like it was, the fallen tree, the stream, he's talking about entering her from behind. He's recreating the murder scene." Britton wasn't so sure.

I'm not surprised. I had chosen a rural setting for our sex session because I love the great outdoors. I was describing a romantic place, not a killing ground.

Meanwhile, they had other problems to deal with. A TV documentary on offender profiling was being made, with particular reference to the Nickell murder. Leading psychologist David Canter – the *real* Cracker, who would later act for my defence – was taking part. He believed he could aid the inquiry, but amazingly, given his expertise in reading murder scenes, had not been invited to help.

The police tried to stop the broadcast. When that failed they got Britton to appear, deflecting interest away from the case by waffling on about profiling in general. (Not hard for him.)

They were also getting frustrated with my responses to Lizzie. It was time to up the ante and push me towards revealing things that only Rachel's killer could know. Lizzie's next letter started:

With you I am starting to feel re-born. Your lovely fantasy letter was absorbing, I only hope these were your genuine thoughts and what you really think about us.

I want it to be private and true, not the kind of usual story that everyone reads in magazines. My fantasies hold no bounds. My imagination runs riot. Sometimes this worries me and it would be nice if sometimes you have the same unusual dreams as me.

Sometimes I scare myself with what I really want. I hope I'm not sounding unnatural, that sometimes normal things just aren't enough and my demands are greater, not just straight sex, there is so much more to explore. (God! Please don't think I'm a weirdo.)

Sexually people do not use their imagination, but I'm sure you do and can. Colin my darling you are driving me mad and I love your letters. Tell me something that will really send me crazy.

I want to feel like I want to burst. Don't worry about upsetting me. I'm sure you can never do that. I constantly think of the letter you wrote about our first meeting, where you took charge of the situation.

You were manly and really showed me who was the boss. I need someone, strong and powerful, your letters are so direct I know you must be too.

As later became clear, while I was swallowing Lizzie's bait hook, line and sinker, Britton was telling the police that I should be given complete freedom of response. He predicted I would act in one of three ways. I would either:

1) *Withdraw from the relationship because the prospect of a sexual liaison based on domination and degradation would be unacceptable to him;*

2) *Indicate his enjoyment of such things in a private relationships, but this would be at a level no different from that of many consenting adults whose sex life is spiced up with symbolic exchanges of sexual control and submission, even sometimes involving restraints;*

3) *Attempt to develop a relationship with Lizzie that increasingly focused on physically and sexually violent fantasies that included her, and would ultimately comprise the most serious kinds of sexual assault.*

His conclusion was that if I opted for choices one or two I would eliminate myself. But if I chose number three the operation would still be up and running. As he explained:

Anybody who chose the latter option, if he had been responsible for the murder of Rachel Nickell, would find the sexual excitement and expectation arising from these violent fantasies so great, that in due course, it could override his caution.

Ultimately, the killer would be likely to disclose his guilt to someone he believed was a confidante, particularly if he felt such a disclosure would be part of an even greater sexual gratification.

Cutting through this bullshit, he was in effect saying that anyone who went along with her request for more violent fantasy scenes fitted the killer's profile exactly. What planet was he living on? Having seen a picture of this gorgeous, mixed–up woman and swapped sex stories, I doubt there's many blokes anywhere in this world who wouldn't have invented whatever turned her on, if it led to getting their wicked way with her!

The only thing I wouldn't say was "I killed Rachel Nickell." But like so much else in this mad scheme, they overlooked the obvious and believed the psychobabble. Lizzie's next letter followed this theme:

You ask me to explain about how I feel when you write your special letters to me. Well, firstly they excite me greatly, but I can't help thinking you are showing great restraint.

You are showing control when you feel like bursting. I want you to burst, I want to feel you all powerful and overwhelming so that I am completely in your power, defenceless and humiliated. These thoughts are sending me into paradise already . . .

I've been waiting to meet you, it's fate, it's all coming together for us Colin. We've only got to overcome one last hurdle, to be complete. I can hardly wait.

Please write soon and remember nothing you will ever say or do will offend me. I know you are a good man, deep down. I hope this letter has cheered you up.

Take care.

Love, Lizzie x.

It's obvious now that she was obeying 'her master's voice' and raising the stakes. She began to hint at some dark secret that affected her outlook on life. In early March she wrote:

I know we get closer and closer, you sound so much like me and I hope that we can be soul mates and share everything.

There are secrets about me that I long to share with someone. Oh Colin! I've got things to tell you that you won't believe. Things that happened to me which have made my outlook totally different in an exciting way.

Things which have changed my urges and responses. Sometimes I feel guilty about the way I feel. You asked me to explain about how I feel when you write your special letters to me.

Well, firstly they excite me greatly, but I can't help but think you are showing great restraint. You are showing control when you feel like bursting. I want you to burst.

I want to feel you all powerful and overwhelming, so that I am completely in your power, defenceless and humiliated. These thoughts are sending me into paradise already.

I was intrigued and excited – as I was meant to be. I may have been sexually inexperienced, except in my fantasies, but I got the hint.

Naturally I wrote back, asking what it was in her past that had given her this totally different outlook. I also included the kind of domination fantasy that she seemed to crave. I was a bit uncomfortable about doing this, but she seemed so keen for me to enter into the spirit of it that I really laid it on. I wrote in my letter of March 18th:

Your letter was great. I now have some idea what you want. I want to be part of you. I want to dominate you, take your body as my plaything. The things I'm going to do to you will literally make your eyes water.

You're right. I do hold back in my 'special' letters. I want to say things to you while abusing your body. I want to call you names in the heat of passion.

I've written another 'special' letter along those lines. I've called you a few dirty names whilst writing it, but please don't think I'm a violent man.

It's just that my passion will take over. You __will__ be left humiliated and dirty. I want to, and will, give you a fucking good sorting out. You need a damn good fucking, by a real man and I am the one to do it.

By the time I'm finished with you you're going to be left sore, exhausted, covered in spunk in every possible hole in your body. I'm going to make you work hard for me. You will be my sex-slave.

I'm going to fuck you, not only in the bedroom but also in more exciting places. I know a few places around here where I'm going to take you. You'll feel so apprehensive, but I will have you.

I am the only man in the world who is going to give it to you. I'm going to make sure you're screaming in agony when I abuse you. I'm going to destroy your self-esteem. You'll never look anybody in the eyes again.

You're going to get it all Lizzie. You're going to be so sore darling, you'll probably find it hard to sit down again.

I hope you're not offended by the dirty names I'm calling you. I do not think you are those things because besides our 'sessions' we will be great friends, full of love for each other, and romance.

I repeated my request for one of her own fantasies:

I want every fantasy of yours in my mind. Every 'kinky' detail, every randy thought, anything you want you'll get, by God you will get it, you randy, dirty, bitch.

I remember thinking I might have gone over the top a bit with this one, because I was still unsure exactly what Lizzie wanted. So four days later I posted her an apology:

Firstly, I hope you enjoyed my last letter to you. Is that the kind of thing you wanted? If you found it too offensive, especially me calling you rude names, I can't apologise enough. But that was the impression I got from your last letter.

Knowing me, I probably got it all wrong. Please forgive me if I did. I don't want to jeopardise our new and 'exciting' relationship over my stupidity.

However if that is the kind of thing you want, then I will <u>gladly</u> fill <u>all</u> your needs.

The sex life between us is going to be fantastic and adventurous, but also we'll have a great friendship, full of love and romance, we are so much alike.

I want to know what really makes you hot and sticky, don't worry about thinking I might be put off by some of them.

Anything goes. If you want me to do something to you I <u>will</u> do it. Don't worry I will give you a good sorting out.

It seemed I had got it right, going by her reply:

You don't offend me in the slightest and it's as if we are really starting to communicate.

I think we are the same. It is a long time since I have felt as if I am on the brink of something wonderful as this, Colin.

I so desperately want this and to trust you is the only way, with each letter you write I am closer to that.

Enclosed was a ram's head pendant on a silver chain, which she described as:

The most valuable thing I own, not in terms of price, but in memories and dreams. I have owned it since I was a young girl. It was given to me by special people.

I know it looks a bit creepy, but don't worry about it. This is the key which unlocks me. If you hold dear this thing which is so important to my life, I'm sure you will have experienced the same things as me and these things will have made us the same. I want you to know about the things I have done.

From what she had hinted in earlier descriptions of her personal beliefs, plus the nature of the gift, I thought it had something to do with the occult, possibly black magic. My response was to open up about some of my own beliefs and to try to discover more about her intriguing secret:

I too have certain beliefs. I wasn't going to tell you yet because you might get the wrong idea about me. I will tell you now. I hope these are along the same lines as yours.

I am not a Satanist, or a weirdo as people believe, in fact I am a very down to earth person. What you have done in your life, I want to know everything about you darling, your thoughts, definitely your fantasies.

Please tell me, you're so important in my life now, nothing you say will put me off you, even if you told me you were a 'mass murderer'. I'd still want you in my life, I need you so much my darling.

I also told her how I liked to walk around the house naked because it gave me a sense of freedom, as did nude sunbathing, although I only did that in secluded places. What I didn't admit to her – or to the police when they questioned me later – was that I have always had a high body temperature. I never get cold so I wear the minimum of clothing to keep my body comfortable, even in winter. Loose cut-off T-shirts have long been a favourite; I've never been a stylish person, so my clothes have always been functional. So the tabloids could gloat that I wore 'dodgy looking' singlets, never wore a suit and looked "like a wife beating slob!" This was part of the mental baggage I was carrying as the relationship with Lizzie developed.

There was a bit of farce attached to my next letter. I had included a small gold ring as a present, but explained:

I'm sorry it's a bit out of shape. I bought it for you last week but when I got home I dropped it and accidentally trod on it.

She didn't seem to see the funny side of that.

There was no time for levity back at puppet-master HQ either. Eleven weeks had passed without a significant breakthrough, and they were worried by my increasing requests to meet, or at least phone, Lizzie. It was decided the time had come to make phone contact. She thanked me for the ring and added:

In the past my beliefs have involved other people. I do not see any of these people now and have not done so for some time as certain things we did together made me have mixed feelings about them.

(Don't worry, I'll tell you the full story some day soon) this has made me feel empty and alone. I often reflect on those times.

I was too besotted by my 'dream girl' to find anything suspicious in this behaviour. I went to further extremes to try to please her, to make myself what she wanted from a man, writing her a long letter about my search for someone with the same beliefs:

Am I right in saying you practised sexual rituals? If so, don't worry. I've always wanted to practise sex rites.

The thought of you being with a group of other believers, being naked together and inflicting sexual pleasure to each other makes me excited.

Soon after this, she explained she'd found a job as a cat-sitter for an old lady, and gave me a work number with set times for me to call. I was over the moon. I had been getting so frustrated at the lack of human contact with this sexually adventurous woman. She'd whipped me up into an emotional frenzy, but then somehow seemed to back off and keep me at a distance, hinting she was still unsure if I was the right man for her. Her next letter was a perfect example:

I feel like we are getting so close. I'm worried that we may not be right for each other.

I have met men before that I have felt in tune with, but have been bitterly disappointed. I have only ever met one man before who made me feel complete. This was due to the experiences we shared, these experiences have shaped me today.

I believe I will only ever feel fulfilled again if I meet a man who has the same history as me. The things that happened with this man weren't what normal people would like, these involved upsetting and often hurting people and even though these things are bad I cannot forget how exhilarating they made me feel. I will explain myself better when we speak.

I am at a turning point, you seem so perfect to me that if you fit my criteria there is no going back for us and we will be together forever.

These hints of violence puzzled and disturbed me. I couldn't fully understand what she was getting at. I wrote:

You said in your letter that you and that man used to enjoy hurting and upsetting people. I do not understand, do you mean physically, mentally or emotionally?

Please explain as I live a quiet life too. If I've disappointed you, please do not dump me. Nothing like this has happened to me before. I do not want to lose you. I need you Lizzie.

I want to instil those old feelings you so much yearn for, but please tell me what it is you want, in every detail.

You know what I want Lizzie, but I still do not know what it is you want in this relationship Lizzie. So please darling, tell me.

I was in turmoil at the thought of losing her and made things worse by missing the set time for a phone call. I couldn't get to the call box and her disappointment in me showed. In her next letter she gave a list of set times and dates for me to phone her, and added the following bait:

I've got a lot to get off my chest and I believe in sharing it with you will help me, and make us more together. I've lived with a terrible secret for so long, it's time I worked it through.

We spoke for the first time on April 20th, and for me it was a disaster. At the sound of this sexy Northern accent I got tongue-tied and embarrassed by all the explicit things I had written to her. The conversation was stilted and she did most of the talking. But we agreed to speak again a week later, and this time I felt comfortable enough to suggest a meeting.

She said she didn't know London well and suggested Hyde Park. I don't like crowds, but I agreed because of the prospect of meeting her at last. I was excited by the phone call and wrote her a long letter, outlining for the first time my domestic situation as a result of the Rachel Nickell murder:

A lot has gone on in my life since last year and none of it is my fault. I will tell you what happened but please, please Lizzie do not be like everybody else around here and think I am guilty. You are my only hope. Apart from my dog I have no friends to confide in.

I told her about Rachel's murder and my arrest. But I stressed:

I am not a murderer, as my belief is that all life from the smallest insect to plant, animal and man is sacred and unique.

To destroy a life wantonly is the greatest sin of all. Because I am a loner and I have ancient beliefs (which everybody believes is dabbling in black magic or devil worship, which it is not) the police held me for three days, continually questioning me.

I co-operated with the police in every way, subjected myself and my property to tests which all proved negative. In the end they let me go.

But the main problem is the local people. I've been called names in the street, I've had kids throwing eggs at me and my kitchen window and rumours keep spreading about me.

I was supposed to have tried to smash someone's window on the top floor of a high-rise flat with a large hammer and even worse.

The last rumour I have heard today is that I go out in my garden every midnight stark naked with my arms raised and masturbate myself! For God's sake what are these people trying to do to me?

I know some of my letters do have stories of having sex with you over the common and parks. But please Lizzie, I just have an adventurous outlook on sex. I am not a dangerous person.

Nor am I a weirdo, pervert. I have done none of the things that people have claimed. I was even accused by the police of sacrificing pigeons in my bedroom!

Just because they found a few feathers on my carpet. Their feathers and leaves and stuff just get blown in by the wind.

Anyway Lizzie, if you started to have doubts about me, I understand. But no-one believes I am innocent. I am just a quiet lonely bloke who lives a quiet lonely life with his dog.

I am just easy prey for anything like this. Don't desert me darling I know I've probably made you think twice about me now. I am sorry if you have lost interest. I hope not. I need someone Lizzie.

I am so desperately lonely, so desperately lonely. I need to be hugged. I need the warmth and love of a good woman. The world seems even colder and darker now because of all this.

I won't pressure you Lizzie, if you say it's over I'll leave it at that. I respect your fears and concerns, but believe me Lizzie I am innocent. I love you my darling. Reply very, very soon.

Yours always
Colin

It's plain from the content this was the real me. A pathetic sounding wimp who literally wouldn't hurt a fly. Not exactly what the murder squad and their profiler wanted to hear.

Unsurprisingly, Lizzie didn't drop me – though I didn't know why at the time. Her handlers were about to change the plot in the face of all my pleas of innocence. The stakes were about to get much higher.

SIX

L etters from Lizzie were all I had to look forward to that spring. Although the hate campaign had lost its intensity, the stigma was still there and I took the taunts badly.

The police showed I was still on their radar by an incident on the edge of the common. I had taken Brandy for a walk along with a bag of stale bread and crusts to feed the ducks.

On my way back I met an old chap I knew, out with his dog, and we stopped to chat, just off the road. A police car pulled up and two officious young cops walked up to us. They told the old man to go and, although I asked him to stay and be my witness, he tottered off. Once he was gone they asked me what I was doing. Pointing to my dog, I said, "Take a wild guess."

Then they searched me and found nothing. I wanted them to take me down to their station but they weren't about to go that far. As they walked off they warned me, "We've got our eye on you."

I had always been a loner, but for the first time I was learning what it felt like to be all alone, never knowing who to trust.

Among the few people I did feel safe with were my new next-door neighbours, Cheryl, a cuddly mother of four boys, and her partner Richard.

Perhaps it was because they were new to the estate, but they didn't share most people's prejudice against me. I shared my excitement with them about this wonderful woman who had burst into my life. I even showed them her opening letter. I should have listened to their first reactions.

Both of them were immediately very suspicious. Cheryl said, "Be careful. This could be a police set-up. You don't really know anything about this woman or who she is." Her words were prophetic, but I laughed off Cheryl's worries and ignored her advice. I was too besotted to even consider the warning. I needed the intimacy that Lizzie seemed to promise.

By the first week in May I was getting worked up at the prospect of finally meeting her, and despite their misgivings, Cheryl and Richard shared my excitement. At last, in a phone call on May 7th, Lizzie set a meeting date. It was to be my birthday treat on May 20th. A picnic in Hyde Park.

During that conversation I told her about my latest fantasy letter, which was in the post. I thought she would be pleased with it because I had taken on board what I understood she wanted, and included a lot of rough stuff. I started describing how I used one of my leather belts to smack her bare bum, leaving red marks on her skin. She was lying on my bed in agony while I tied her arms and legs to the corners. Then I fucked her hard and violently before grabbing her hair and using the belt to pull her head back.

Lizzie stopped me there. "Don't tell me any more. You'll spoil the rest of the story for me. I'm looking forward to reading it."

A week later, during another phone chat, she brought up the Nickell murder: "Quite frankly Colin, it wouldn't matter to me if you had murdered her. I'm not bothered. In fact, in certain ways I wish you had because it would make things easier for me 'cause I've got something to tell you.

"I'll tell you on Thursday [May 20th] so that you know, it makes me realise that it was fate that brought us together."

I was intrigued and a bit worried. "Right," I said. "But you know I'm innocent of everything. I haven't done anything, and the things that you're into and that – I mean, I haven't done anything before, and I was wondering if you think we wouldn't hit it off."

She ignored this and said, "Your last letter, well that was really interesting. God knows what the next one's going to be like."

I replied that I wasn't into real violence. "I think all life is sacred."

Her response to that was, "Oh well, I hope you're not going to be shocked by what I've got to tell you. Oh, I'm worried now."

Not for the first time I thought this was a very strange woman, but I didn't give a toss. I wasn't going to miss the chance of bedding this exciting, sexy creature just because she was a bit weird.

The next day, she sent me a 'formal' invitation to our first meeting:

Miss Elizabeth James
cordially invites
Mr Colin Stagg
to Hyde Park
on 20th May 1993, 2pm
for the occasion
of a
birthday picnic.
Be there or be square.

I was to recognise her by her floral dress and Marks and Spencer's carrier bag. She would be standing next to the lamppost outside the Dell café, beside the Serpentine. She added, "PS. I won't keep you too long, so your dog will be all right."

I was over the moon! At last! Our next words would be face to face. And that's when I was manipulated into the endgame of Operation Edzell.

Bear in mind that Paul Britton had stipulated from the start: "For the operation to work, the suspect has to always make the first move. Words can't be put into his head. Lizzie can only react to the cues that he gives."

What happened next gave the lie to that.

My birthday dawned, and the rain was teeming down. The torrent lasted all day. It was another omen I ignored. In those days, I could still use public transport. My fear of being instantly recognisable and getting attacked had yet to fully set in. But I was still nervous riding up to central London on the bus, partly because of the locals' attitude near my home, and also because I was about to meet my dream woman.

After getting off at Hyde Park Corner, I realised I was over an hour early. So, despite the rain, I went for a walk around the lake. Even in the rain, I kept thinking that people were staring at me – only later did I discover that 'they' were the police.

I put it down to nerves, but instead of waiting in the café I killed time, standing under a big oak tree, sheltering from the rain in the open air. At last a lone woman approached the café under an umbrella. I couldn't see her dress because of her raincoat, but when she stopped outside I decided it must be her.

As I approached she turned round and said very softly, "You must be Colin." I was bowled over. She was lovely. "And you must be Lizzie," was all I could think of saying as we went inside. Gorgeous shoulder-length blonde hair, blue eyes. And when I helped her off with her coat I could see she had a beautiful figure. She looked stunning.

We sat down and ordered some fish and chips and two small bottles of wine. Before our meal arrived she produced some birthday presents for me, something nobody outside my family had ever done. There was a Walkman stereo, a baseball cap and a joke birthday card featuring two chimps, one of who had a big erection.

It made us laugh – although I was feeling awkward, and must have sounded dead boring. Then she revealed her big secret and nothing was boring anymore. As we ate, she talked about having been groomed by a witchcraft group between the ages of twelve and eighteen. They had introduced her to group sex with members of the coven.

The high spot of her sex-fuelled black magic 'apprenticeship' came ten years previously, when she took part in the ritual killing of a mother and her newborn baby. I was dumbfounded. I could only sit in silence as she described how it had sexually excited her like nothing else in her life. When she told me about the killings she closed her eyes, and seemed to be having an orgasm.

I didn't know what to say at first. What *could* I say? I'd had a suspicion that her secret had involved some sort of satanic ritual, but nothing like baby murder or human sacrifice. This was completely off the wall and very disturbing.

It felt so unreal, sitting there in a damp, steamy café in Hyde Park, with rain streaming down the window beside us, opposite this weird and wonderful woman who might be describing a scene straight out of *Tales from the Crypt*.

I remember Lizzie breaking off her story to ask me, "I'm not putting you off your dinner, am I?" I know it sounds stupid, but all I could think to say was, "The fish is a bit cold, but the chips are alright. Carry on."

They were eventually able to use that against me as proof of my cold-bloodedness.

She went on, as recorded on the Metropolitan Police's surveillance tapes. "Well this baby, erm, had its throat cut and it was just . . . it was a brand-new baby and I think it had just been born by one of these other girls.

"This is just what I can remember at the time, being so shocked and I mean I . . . but it was so hard to say. It didn't look awful but it was shocking.

"It was hard to say, and then the baby's, erm, blood was put into a cup and everybody had a drink of this and it was the most electrifying atmosphere and I was, I was, I don't know how can I describe it. It was like mixed, mixed feelings, you know, they were all like as if they were really drunk.

"Well this woman was sort of laid out on this thing and, erm, she was naked and erm, these knives were brought out and she, it was as if she knew what was happening, you know, and she just lay there and he came round in the room, this man, and handed me one of the knives.

"And he asked me to cut the woman's throat, and then I did and took the cup, and with the cup I caught the woman's blood, and then I don't know what happened with her, but there was this big orgy and I was with this man, well this man was the best ever. It was the best thing I could ever imagine. The best sex ever!"

Afterwards, she apparently had mixed feelings about what had happened and what she had done. Finally, she withdrew from the group and moved away. But from then on she came to believe that only a man with similar experiences could truly satisfy her. She had tried to form relationships with other men, but they fizzled out because they lacked that vital ingredient.

Her years with the coven had left her with a very strong

interest in extreme sex and sexual fantasies, which was why she thought I could be 'the one' for her.

I was trying to make sense of what she was saying. It sounded fantastical, but it would explain why she switched back and forth from being so wild yet so wary. Perhaps it wouldn't have sounded so farfetched if I'd known something of Mr Britton and his background at the time. It would certainly give me pause for thought years later.

I have also since discovered that Paul Britton is an evangelical Christian. Without decrying his faith, it strikes me that a man with such traditional beliefs might not be best disposed towards a follower of paganism like me. It may be coincidental, but he may have regarded me as someone likely to be involved in ritualistic crime, like in all those discredited 'satanic abuse' stories back in the late 1980s and early 1990s.

I mention this merely to show how Britton could get things wrong. He got it wrong with me. He may even have got it wrong in November 1993, when a mother and child were frenziedly stabbed to death in south London and Britton insisted there was no link with the murder of Rachel Nickell.

But that day in Hyde Park, I was trying my best to get my head around this chilling admission and how best to respond. All I could say was, "I've got an open mind about everything, I mean everybody's got a secret in their past, ain't they? But I couldn't do anything like that. I have my beliefs but they don't involve human sacrifices."

Looking back on it now, her story was more like *Carry on up the Crypt*. It seems ludicrous. Even then I was in two minds whether to take her seriously. But, sitting at that table, I decided to go along with her. After all, I was a bit of a weirdo myself – according to popular opinion – and she was too good looking to give up. I decided to see where it all led.

Straight to the dock of the Old Bailey, as it happened. Still, there was no hint of that as we walked arm in arm to the park gates and she hailed a taxi. Just as she got in, I handed her another fantasy letter I had written specially for the occasion of meeting her at last.

It would get the police all excited, because I had written it before learning the details of Lizzie's 'violent past'. It also carried a warning from me that it involved danger. What had them positively drooling was that I'd included the use of a knife for the first time. It was only used as a prop in my story, but to them it reinforced Britton's profile of the killer.

Once again the setting was the common, on a hot sunny afternoon. Lizzie and I find a secluded spot, strip off and lie down on a towel. As we start fondling each other I notice a man watching us from behind a tree.

It's a turn-on. So I encourage Lizzie to put on a show by saying loudly, "Suck me off." He watches while I push her over a tree trunk and have rear-entry sex while secretly motioning the stranger to approach. He strips and comes up behind her. Then I pull out of her and invite him to take my place, while I force my cock into her mouth. She loves having us both at the same time.

The fantasy continues with him suggesting something dangerous, and she agrees. He goes back to his clothes and returns with a knife and some rope. We grab Lizzie and tie her down, spread-eagled. I wrote:

The man sits astride you, his cock still dripping spunk onto your belly. He gently takes the blade of the knife and draws it down gently from your breasts to your cunt, not cutting you, just teasing you.

Then I place the blade under his cock and squeeze a few drops of spunk onto the blade, then he places it in your mouth and makes you lick it clean, which you do.

You are now so hot and red you are panting excitedly. The man then cuts himself on his arm, just enough to draw blood and he drips it onto your nipples.

You massage it into your breasts, making you rock your head backwards and forwards and sideways as you go into a massive orgasm.

I went on to describe both of us going on to have rough sex with her, which included pulling her hair and putting the knife against her cheek and teasing her nipples with it. The letter ends with me asking if she's happy with the content:

I hope that was to your satisfaction Lizzie. Don't worry. I'll make sure no harm will come to you, while you're with me. I've written this story along the lines of what I feel you are into. If I've frightened you please tell me. I don't want to upset you, you're special darling.

DI Pedder was ecstatic. I had mentioned a knife, cutting flesh and blood. He couldn't wait to fax the letter through to Britton for analysis. "So where does this latest fantasy put Stagg?" was his key question. His only concern was the use of the words 'defenceless and humiliated' – which they had used in a Lizzie letter back in March. Britton replied:

We allowed him freedom of expression, so the themes in this last letter are far too extreme to have been prompted. No, they have been spontaneously generated.

There were endless other sexual liaisons and escapades he could have envisaged and written about, yet he chose this narrow and quite specific pathway of his own accord.

It's consistent with what I would expect to find in the masturbatory repertoire of the killer. It also has the various elements known to be relevant to the murder of Rachel Nickell.

You are looking at someone with a highly deviant sexuality that's present in a very small number of men in the general population.

As I've said before the chances of two such men being on Wimbledon Common when Rachel was murdered are vanishingly small.

He added that a large number of people have sex lives which include elements of coercion, bondage or sadism.

If this was all, Mr Stagg would have eliminated himself from the investigation. Instead he went beyond this and showed arousal at a tiny and specific strand of fantasy.

It featured violence, rape and sexual pain. This had been predicted of the killer months before Stagg ever became a suspect.

Now I'm no psychologist, but I'd have thought a threesome – 'fucking and sucking' – was a fairly common men's fantasy. I'm an outdoors bloke, so it should have been no surprise I'd choose an open-air scenario. As for the use of a knife, I thought that's what she'd been hinting at, and I'd only used it 'gently'. I even stressed afterwards I would never hurt her. There was no suggestion of rape, and I even apologised if the fantasy had frightened her.

But that simple explanation didn't fit. These were highly experienced men in their different fields, at the top of their game. Yet they only saw what they wanted to see. Nothing could interfere with their master-plan. If something seemed to fit then they ignored any alternative.

This is clearly demonstrated by my next letter, on May 22nd. I had phoned Lizzie the day after her 'confession'. She still insisted that she could only have a true relationship with a man who had done something like that. I pleaded with her:

Lizzie I've never done that kind of thing. I mean what you told me and that, if I did do that I would have told you that I'd done it, 'cause I know I could have trusted you.

Her response on the phone was a bit snappish. "Oh well, I'm going to have to think about this."

That got me worried. "You're going to turn me down, aren't you?" I whined.

She ignored that, and switched the subject to Rachel's murder and my supposed involvement. "If only it had been true," she said softly.

"I'm sorry if I'm not the one for you then, Liz. I was hoping I was."

The conversation petered out with us agreeing to "think about things". I walked home from the phone box feeling low and dejected.

Next day, I wrote to Lizzie describing how down I felt at the prospect of losing her. I also said:

I could have lied to you about the murder, and say I did it, just to be with you. I wish you felt the same way about me.

But I felt so sad and miserable after posting it that I just had to come up with a plan to rekindle her interest in me. It was pathetic, really. But you have to remember that I thought this woman was my soulmate, and I'd have done anything to keep her.

So in a phone call to her on May 25th, I came up with this story of how, as a twelve-year-old schoolboy, my cousin and I had murdered a little girl in the woods, and hid her body while we were on a caravanning holiday in the New Forest:

We noticed this little boy and a little girl sitting on the edge of the forest and that and the little boy ran off playing and we took the little girl into the forest and we ended up, it wasn't nothing really that perverted, it was just, you know we ended up killing her, you know strangling her.

The reason we never got done for it was 'cos we were leaving that same evening. But the thing was, when we was actually strangling her, we felt exactly the same feelings that you described to me. Everything was buzzing you know, we were just floating, the whole experience was just floating.

I added that I hadn't told her before because I had hoped we could have a relationship without me having to disclose my own 'dark secret'. It was utter nonsense then and it sounds even more stupid now. But although she said, "It doesn't make us the same, does it?", she did suggest another meeting. That lifted my spirits.

The police only had to make one call to the Hampshire force for my story to be revealed as a total fantasy. But Paul Britton still managed to extract some juice from it. "He may have interwoven some details of the Rachel Nickell murder into this fictional account," he told Lizzie. "You should get into the habit of asking him questions about the murder.

"Ask him how he felt when it happened. Make him see how you need to know if his experience really does parallel yours. Get him used to talking about the details.

"That way, if he eventually reveals himself to be Rachel's killer, he's not going to be surprised when Lizzie asks him lots of detailed questions, looking for the proof."

So over our next few phone calls she teased some more details out of me. I tried to put her off by saying I would tell her when we were 'going steady'. It was all I could think of.

But she kept on about it at our second meeting. It was in Hyde Park again, on June 4th, and this time it was a lovely hot day. There were crowds of people so I almost didn't find her.

We sat in deckchairs beside the Serpentine and drank cans of cheap wine. When she asked how the little girl's murder had made me feel I admitted, "That's what makes me feel guilty about it, because I enjoyed it. You know, your whole body felt like it was buzzing, everything kind of high." That was the best I could do.

She sounded sceptical. "Your story is very vague. I've told you I don't even feel guilty about what I did. I've told you everything, and mine wasn't just one childish murder. It's as if you don't trust me, you're just telling me half a story. I want you to tell me more.

"I want you to reassure me. I need to know it's the truth. I don't want to hear stuff like, 'We were twelve.'"

She was dismissive of my boyhood killing in comparison with her own. "It's like a schoolboy game gone wrong. That's not what I'm after. The feelings that you got from that are totally different. You're living in the guilt of a mistake. I'm living in the glory of it!"

We bickered for a bit longer and threw bread at the ducks. When we were saying goodbye I tried to kiss her cheek, but she turned away. We parted after I promised to phone.

I sent her some more letters over the next few weeks and we chatted on the phone. She was still a bit distant, and kept telling me she knew I was holding back and that it was vital for our relationship to open up to her.

I was starting to feel despondent. We seemed to be getting nowhere, and I couldn't understand exactly what she wanted.

But when a small parcel arrived from Lizzie on June 24th, my mood brightened. It was a cassette tape, and at long last she was giving me a sex fantasy of her own!

SEVEN

There's nothing like a woman talking dirty to turn a man on. Lizzie was so good at it, she could have made a fortune on a sex chat line.

Perhaps I would have been less excited if I'd known her tape was really a carefully worded reflection of my own stories, put together by some beefy coppers! And as always it had been approved and directed by my hidden manipulator, Paul Britton.

The tape started out like a romantic Barbara Cartland bodice-ripper, but swiftly moved into graphic hardcore porn. Her fantasy described us walking hand in hand through woodland on a hot summer's day. "I am getting sticky," she says in that sexy northern accent of hers.

Your tender grip reveals the same. It is not only my hand that is getting sticky!

You lead me further into the woods. I know you want some privacy from prying eyes and I am happy to be led by you.

At last you stop. I can see by that masterful look in your eye that this is the time. You pull me towards you and my heart races, your tongue pushes into my willing hungry mouth and we taste each other.

I immediately feel overcome by your masculinity and you sink to your knees, drawing me down with you. Your strong hands hold my firm buttocks. I can feel your manhood straining to be released from your jeans as you lie on top of me.

Your hands are now pulling at my top, my breasts are also straining to be released. In your haste to release them my top rips. It excites me even more and I can feel that special wetness between my legs.

I claw at your T-shirt pulling it up at the back. You let me rake your firm, muscular back. I am filled with an animal passion and begin to beg you to fill me up. You tell me to shut up and wait. You have other things on your mind.

You pull open my skirt and pull it down. The cool air hits my cunt like an electric shock as you pull my legs wide. "Wank yourself!" you shout. "Show me what's on offer!"

I start pushing my finger into my wet hole. I look into your eyes. There is a look of total, utter control. As I push a second finger into my pink slot I can smell myself as a cool breeze passes over me.

The musky smell of a woman's sex. I know you can smell me too as your nostrils flare in appreciation. The bulge I can see in your jeans is almost frightening, surely they must burst.

This wonderful thought is suddenly disrupted by a sharp noise. My eyes widen in panic and I quickly search for what has caused it.

I see a young woman about ten yards away. She is about nineteen with a shapely body and short blonde hair, she looks as startled as I am, then I realise why – she has her right hand down the front of her shorts which are unbuttoned.

The image of her fingers in her tight pink cunt suddenly comes to my mind and I smile to myself. I follow her gaze. She is staring at you. You return her gaze, but unblinking and strong. "Don't worry about her!"

you say to me. "I know what she needs." "Join us if you like," you say to her.

She comes over. "Hi! I hope I'm not disturbing you. I couldn't resist a little look." "You carry on love, I want to watch you warm up," you mutter.

"You stand up and move a few feet away. Feel her cunt it's nice and wet for you," you say to our new playmate.

She leans forward, bending to my crotch and she plants a soft wet kiss on my brush. I grab her small, firm tits which are pushing at her T-shirt and pinch her nipples with my thumb and forefingers.

I pull her top off and move up above her. She is beneath me on her back. I pull down her shorts in one swift movement. A quick glance tells me she is a natural blonde.

I work my right hand into her gash, roughly pushing her clitoris from side to side. I can hear the unmistakable sound of a zip being yanked. I look to see you pull out your powerful piece of meat.

It quickly distracts me from what I am doing with our visitor. With one hand you are pulling your cock and with the other you reach behind you and pull something out from where it is tucked in the back of your jeans.

I get a shock: you are holding a knife. To see your hands on two powerful swords really makes me pant. You must have noticed by the look of surprise. "Which prick do you prefer?" you joke.

I smile and touch my pussy again. I have forgotten the girl. You have me under your spell. You stand up, completely removing your jeans. Your massive meaty cock sways slightly with the movement.

I can't keep my eyes off you. You walk over to us and speak to the girl. "Suck me!" She looks at me then you and she doesn't need asking again.

She is on her knees lapping you up. You hold the knife tip against her bright stiff nipples and gently circle one of them with it.

It slowly darkens and a small trail of blood begins to dribble down. She hardly notices, she is feasting on your cock. I frig myself mercilessly. "Come here you bitch, it's your turn," you say to me.

I quickly respond. "Get on your knees," you order. I am only too *willing to oblige you. I feel your muscular hands on my quivering arse and with one powerful thrust you are in me.*

You are so strong you knock me forward off balance. I reach out and grasp at the girl in front. I touch her tits and feel the sticky blood on my hand. I lick it off, smelling it as I do.

Meanwhile you are pounding your length into my softly wet cunt. I can barely take your size. It feels like you are a well-oiled machine, a piston moving perfectly in and out of me.

I feel your meaty cock end swell and it sends me over the edge. "Come you bitch!" you shout at me.

I can no longer take it and all the strength in my legs goes. At last I can feel you explode as my own ecstasy is washing over me, I feel gallons of your seed pumping into.

"Well, you got what you wanted!" you say to me and I collapse forward with you on top of me. My face nestles into the grass. I feel you pull out of me and your cock leaves a sticky snail's trail across my arse.

You hold me in your arms and we drift off to sleep, the girl forgotten by us both. I wake later and it is dusk. You are next to me but the other girl is gone.

I can't remember her face and wonder if I dreamt our crazed session. But then I notice the stickiness on my hand, now going brown, and the shining blade of your knife next to us. You smile and say nothing — we understand each other.

Well, Colin you've waited long enough. I hope you enjoyed it. See you soon.

This tape left me panting. I played it over and over again. What a sexpot! She must have liked me and my stories, after all. It was the green light to carry on writing in the way that seemed to turn her on.

I phoned Lizzie up to thank her for the brilliant tape. She said she was glad I liked it and was especially keen to know if I'd enjoyed the knife-play. "I liked it all," I told her, too excited to notice her fixation.

Three weeks later, on June 29th, we had our third meeting in the park. Once again we sat in deckchairs. I handed her one of my special letters as I opened a bottle of wine and poured into a couple of paper cups I'd brought along.

She was in a playful mood and delighted in reading it out loud, much to my embarrassment. I tried to stop her but she just carried on, enjoying my discomfort.

My story entailed the kidnap and sexual abuse of a wealthy businessman's daughter, Lizzie, who would be held at knifepoint and raped from behind. Too many people could overhear what she was reading. (More than I knew. There were about thirty undercover officers watching us.)

Lizzie steered our conversation back to the subject of Rachel Nickell, and how the police still suspected me. "I wish you had done it," she said wistfully. "Knowing you'd got away with it. I'd think that's brilliant. I wish you had. Screw 'em!"

She was becoming less subtle in her attempts to get a confession out of me, but I didn't notice. I was too busy trying to concoct suitable stories to keep her interested in me. One line I came up with was that I'd really been on the common at the time of the murder. It was a lie. So was telling her I'd got an erection when they showed me the picture of Rachel's dead body.

I was saying anything I could think of to keep her interested. As she seemed keen to hear about the murder on the common, I searched my mind for gory details. Unfortunately I made the assertion that Rachel had been raped and almost beheaded. I really believed she had been. There was something about the photo they showed me, something about the position of the head that gave me that impression.

Lizzie seemed fascinated and wanted to know more and more.

I told her Rachel had been stabbed forty-nine times and was naked when they found her, covered in blood. "In the photograph she was lying down on the grass, sort of curled up. But the photo was taken from sort of her backside upwards, and her head was sort of round and there was blood all over the grass.

"She was completely naked, and from that viewpoint I could see her cunt and you know, she was very wide open, so he must have really forced her open.

"At that time, he was obviously killing her at the time, the muscles, you know, in her body, made her stay open."

Lizzie lapped it all up and asked me details about my arrest, and how the police had questioned me about my times on the common. It all fascinated her. And the more interested she got, the more I babbled on, saying anything that came into my head.

We were there for hours and she seemed relaxed and happy with me. But when we got up to go and I tried to kiss her goodbye, she once again turned her head.

I phoned her a couple of times over the next few days, and she kept turning the conversation back to Rachel. She wanted me to take her to the murder site and "do the things that man did to her" in a sort of perverted re-enactment.

I promised I would, but explained that I never carried a knife on the common and that I couldn't harm anyone with it. She suggested that she carry the knife, and to keep her happy I agreed to it, although I had no intention of going through with any violent ritual.

But Lizzie wouldn't have been worried about that. She was too busy being congratulated by her handlers, who believed I'd at last given away what they called 'guilty knowledge' only the murderer could have known.

Britton was convinced this was the vital breakthrough the operation had been designed to make. A single image, numbered

KP27, had been carefully chosen during my interrogation to show me Rachel's body, but little detail of the murder wounds or injuries. According to him it was "A scene-establishing shot" because it only showed her back and half-naked lower body curled up on the grass. What it didn't show were her neck, hands, face or genitalia.

He was convinced I had described injuries and other details that I couldn't possibly have gleaned from the image I was shown. Britton stated, "He described how Rachel had almost been decapitated even though he couldn't have seen her neck. He said that she lay curled up like a baby and he could see her genitalia which were 'very wide open you know so he must have forced her open.'

"This description graphically and precisely matched the condition of Rachel's anus, yet from examination of the single photograph labelled KP27, Stagg couldn't have known such a detail unless it was a guess.

"He referred to her vagina rather than her anus, but sexually inexperienced men often confuse the two and merge them in their thoughts."

And Britton made the point that not many people would realise muscles don't contract after death, which is why Rachel's anus was still dilated.

They believed I was so taken with Lizzie that I'd forgotten to be cautious, and was almost ready to confess all to her.

When I phoned her the next day we discussed the murder again, and this time I pretended I'd been turned on by the photo of the body. Britton would interpret this as "entirely consistent with the extremely rare and serious sexual deviation that Stagg had already shown".

But even the best of plans can't anticipate everything, and a big spanner was about to be thrown in their wheel.

During that early summer, while I was courting Lizzie, I was still being hassled. Local kids kept on calling me names and shouting abuse. A lot of people still gave me the cold shoulder, and the press also began to pester me again, looking for new material as the anniversary of the murder approached.

I hadn't mentioned the journalists to Lizzie, so her team had no warning when I suddenly decided to give the most polite of them, Nick Constable, an exclusive. I didn't ask for a penny, as I thought it would put the rest off. (Of course it didn't. The ones I turned away just made up whatever they wanted.) But at least the *Daily Star* exclusive put my side of the story, and may even have shown me in a better light – if only briefly.

Unbeknownst to me, Britton had estimated that their operation should take between two and sixteen weeks, depending on my responses to Lizzie and her letters. In fact it had lasted exactly six months, without producing a shred of hard evidence, and might have gone on for months longer. It was only halted in July because of the *Daily Star* interview protesting my innocence.

The front-page headline read, "I didn't kill Rachel Nickell" above a big picture of me. If that wasn't bad enough, they suddenly realised the picture also clearly showed a photo of Lizzie (one she had sent me) on the mantelpiece. They were afraid some reporter would discover the truth and use it to identify her.

I only did the interview to try to stop the malicious gossip, and because Constable was the one member of the press up until then to treat me like a human being. Although a lot of the badmouthing had died down, I was still being called 'murderer' and 'killer'. I hoped I could stop it by putting my side in print.

The police were in despair. Pedder, Wickerson and Lizzie were on their way to a conference with Britton on July 5th when they picked up the paper at motorway services. They were devastated

Months of undercover work hadn't produced a single item of

hard evidence. Other than a lot of smutty fantasies I had been invited to write, they had nothing concrete on me. Even what they apparently saw as 'guilty knowledge' of the murder scene could be explained as guesswork on my part.

Now they feared that the *Star* article would generate a lot of calls and letters from women sympathetic to my plight, who might be a lot more willing than Lizzie to have sex. But Britton was more upbeat. He suggested Lizzie should divert my attention by showing how upset she was by my story.

It worked. When I phoned her later that day she acted furious. She laid into me for "getting involved with the press" and inadvertently putting her picture into the paper. She warned me it had damaged our whole relationship as she was concerned that I might blab about her.

As a peace offering – so I thought – I sent her another fantasy letter to cheer her up. In light of her repeated interest in the Rachel Nickell killing, I set the scene on Wimbledon Common. In it, Lizzie is a long-legged blonde who has oral and rear-entry sex with me and a mystery man, which concludes with a knife blade being used to trigger her orgasm.

Britton's conclusion was: "The female participant in this fantasy, described by Stagg as Lizzie James, is accurate of Rachel Nickell.

"The sexual fantasy focuses on aggressive rear-entry sexual intercourse with the involvement of an additional male.

"In this fantasy Mr Stagg depicts himself as receiving equivalent sexual pleasure from penile intercourse and the use of the knife in a physically aggressive manner.

"I regard this as further evidence of serious sexual deviance and would expect it to be entirely consistent with the major elements in the fantasy themes of the person who murdered Rachel Nickell."

So there! Such a simple solution! Elementary, my dear

Britton. Despite how Lizzie had made it crystal clear she enjoyed playing with knives, when I used that theme in my stories it made me a killer.

I followed up with two more fantasy phone calls over the next few days, which she seemed to enjoy, and we arranged to meet on July 20th.

The day before, Lizzie met with Pedder and Britton for a strategy discussion. It was agreed that she should now use, in Britton's words, "a combination of positive attraction and appropriate reserve". Up until then, the Lizzie connection had provided them with neither a confession nor a murder weapon. But Pedder and Britton felt I had provided a lot of circumstantial evidence that fitted Britton's profile like a glove.

Would they have enough to charge me? Our next meeting, which was to prove our last, would provide the answer.

Hyde Park again. 11.35am, earlier than before. We settled down under a beech tree in sight of the Dell Café and the lake. Each of us carried a copy of the *Star* article.

The ground was damp so I gave Lizzie my jacket to sit on. She had bought two cans of white wine for us. As we drank, she asked if I had written one of my 'specials'. I apologised but promised to send one on to her.

Almost immediately, she turned the conversation around to my arrest and what had happened to me. I described being held for three days, and how they took blood, saliva and hair samples without any of them yielding a result. I explained they had spent a lot of time trying to break me down, but they couldn't because I was telling the truth. I mentioned that the only evidence – if you could call it that – came from some women who thought they had seen me on the common at the time of the murder.

Then she turned her attention to the newspaper article and

encouraged me to dig my own grave. Pointing to my copy, she asked why some paragraphs were circled in biro. "That's where they got it wrong," I replied.

She read on, then added, "'Cos they said in the paper that you said you weren't there at the time, but you told me you had been."

She had picked up on the lie I'd told to impress her at our previous meeting. I had to pretend it was the truth. Everything was getting twisted. "I had to say that to the paper. I'd told the police, you know, I wasn't there at the time," I told her.

"Oh, yeah," she replied.

Conversation flagged when I tried to touch her knee and kiss her. She pulled away both times. I felt I was losing her.

"I want someone like the man who did this thing. He fascinates me. I think about him and I try and imagine it and the thought of him is so exciting," she said, returning again to the murder theme.

"I wish it was me who'd done it, you know," I replied. "'Cos I mean, I feel guilty about the thought, you know, it does turn me on a lot. It did right from the beginning."

"But what bits turned you on? What were the bits that really, you know, turned you on? Seeing the dead body or imagining it, what was it?" she asked.

"Things that he did, that he was actually having sex with her at the same time, forcing himself into her," I replied. I felt a bit sick saying something like this, but the more perverted I sounded the more she lapped it up. I wanted to keep her interested.

"Is that what he did?" asked Lizzie.

"That's what he must have done. Yeah. But I mean he must. He probably went just crazy while he was fucking her, 'cos she was stabbed forty-nine times, something like that," I added. "If you think about it, if he just suddenly attacked her, right, it was a knife that stabbed her, and he gets a big hard-on like, you know, he's getting really aroused and that, then obviously he's gonna force himself into her, ain't he, while he's doing it? I mean, she'd be struggling and the more she struggles, you know, the more it's all a turn-on."

"Yeah, but if he stabbed her she might have been dead anyway."

"Depends where he stabbed her first."

"Didn't they tell you where he'd stabbed her first?"

"No, all I know is that he stabbed her forty-nine times. You know, her head was decapitated."

"Why did he do that?"

"Probably just trying to cut her head off."

Then Lizzie picked on what I'd said at our previous meeting about Rachel being 'wide open'. Although I didn't really want to discuss it again, she wouldn't let up.

"You say she was gaping wide open?"

"Yeah."

"What, her genitals?"

"Yeah."

I tried to show her exactly how the body had looked from what I could remember of the photograph, almost a year after I had seen it. Putting my palms on the ground, I lowered myself down on my left side and curled myself round into a sort of foetal position, knees bent and legs drawn up.

This small physical movement was to prove a crucial factor in putting me in the dock. I had put my hands out side by side; Lizzie later insisted that I had put my hands together as if in prayer, which was how the police claimed her body was found.

It was to be a pivotal part of the evidence against me that the photograph I'd seen did *not* show the position of Rachel's hands. Only the murderer could have known exactly how her hands were positioned.

(At trial, after studying photos that did show the hands' true position, the judge stressed they were not palm to palm but crossed at the wrist.)

At the time, I was merely trying to keep Lizzie's interest by whatever means possible. So when she next asked if I "could see right up her", I showed her what I thought I'd seen, cupping my hands to indicate an open vagina as best I could. When she asked if this was her "fanny or her arsehole", I replied, "Her fanny."

Lizzie still wouldn't give up. "Your letters to me get more and more explicit, and to me that's fantastic. I just wish they were real. I just wish you had done lots of things like me." She kept pressing me to admit that I was the killer, and showed disappointment when I kept denying it.

"I've been thinking little fantasies that perhaps you are the man that did it. Perhaps you don't want to tell me the reasons, but fair do's, perhaps you are that man.

"I want to go over there. I want to see where it happened. I want you to show me and I want you to treat me sort of like that man treated her. I want all that.

"But if you're not that man and haven't done that kind of thing, you'll never, ever be able to fulfil me. You'll never, Colin. Never.

"And now I'm going to live my whole life like this, time and time again, hurt."

I thought she was deranged! "Maybe we should call it a day," I said miserably.

"I'm going to have to go," she said. "I'm gonna get too upset if I stay here any longer. I don't want you to see me cry."

"Do you want me to ring you?" I asked.

"It's up to you. It's up to you. I'm gonna have to go. Bye." And with that, she picked up her things and walked off across the park. I watched until she was out of sight, then sadly dusted down my jacket and headed for home. I felt so low.

Next day I phoned and begged her to reconsider dumping me, but she insisted I wasn't the right man for her after all, and asked me to return her letters.

I wrote to her again, telling her how lonely I felt:

Oh Lizzie, I wish, I wish so much that I was that murderer. I wish I was the man for you.

A week after our meeting I returned her tape. Lizzie wrote back, thanking me and saying how upset she was that I hadn't proved to be 'the one' for her. She apologised for hurting me in any way and indicated that she might be going to America in the near future. She ended by saying she'd like to see me one last time in Hyde Park.

But I couldn't face any more heartbreak. On August 10th, exactly twenty-nine weeks after it began, I effectively ended Operation Edzell by saying "there's no point" and admitting I had lied to her about killing a little girl in the New Forest. My last words were, "But I just didn't want to lose you. I will always miss you, darling. I haven't felt randy since we broke up."

This wasn't quite true – although it was certainly our last contact until after I was arrested for the murder of Rachel Nickell.

But at the time, I began to wonder whether losing Lizzie wasn't a bad thing. Although I loved the sexual fantasies with her, she was just a bit too wild and flaky for someone as tame as me. After six months of emotional highs and lows, I wanted to get some sort of normality back in my life. As luck would have it, a couple of new romantic opportunities had arisen.

Since the big newspaper article and my last meeting with Lizzie, a woman from Wales had started writing to me. She was also into sexual fantasy. Janet George, who lived in Swansea, had read my story and felt sorry for me because, she said, she'd had similar problems with the police in her past.

Like Lizzie she began to write very explicit letters, although they didn't come anywhere near the same weird desires. Janet's were far more down-to-earth and dirty. It was easy for me to respond in kind after all the practice I'd had. I sent her seven letters in total.

And suddenly there was the very real prospect of some 'nooky', literally on my own doorstep. Lynda lived in the flat above mine. She had two children and, although they'd split up, she still shared the place with the kids' father while he looked for new digs.

Lynda was one of the few neighbours who hadn't joined the witch-hunt against me. She was in her late twenties, still trim, with a good figure and nice smile. I'd confided in her when I started to lose Lizzie and she was very sympathetic. Then somehow we got a lot closer. She visited my flat a couple of times and we enjoyed a kiss and a cuddle. It was obvious that, sooner or later, we were going to have sex.

It so happened we had arranged for her to come down to my place on the evening of August 17th. She had been very flirty with me and I was sure this was going to be the night. So I celebrated in advance the previous evening, with a couple of bottles of cider. That made me tipsy and I fell asleep early on the couch.

But my boozy dreams were rudely shattered by a hammering on the front door.

It was 5am, the time Russians used to call 'the KGB hour', because that was when the secret police usually staged their raids. I stumbled into the hall half asleep. "Who's there?" I called out.

"Police!" came the reply. "Open up!"

As the door swung back I was confronted by a poker-faced DI

Pedder, with a crowd of cops behind him. He allowed himself a thin smile as he flashed his warrant card and recited those dreadful words: "I'm arresting you for the murder of Rachel Nickell."

Panic set in. All I could think to say was, "You must be joking!" as the officers piled into my home. I was in a daze.

In the living room I managed a bit of defiance. "You're setting me up for this!" I said to Pedder. That got to him. Pointing at me, he growled, "Listen, you. I've never set anybody up in my life."

I didn't believe him at the time, but, strangely, since then I've come to think he was telling the truth. He wanted Rachel's killer so badly he just seized the only straw offered by the undercover operation. Thanks to Paul Britton, he genuinely came to believe the Lizzie letters proved my guilt beyond all doubt. He thought he'd finally got his man.

All I could think about, as they led me out in handcuffs to the police car, was who was going to take care of my dog?

Despite the early hour, curtains were twitching and people came out onto the balconies to watch me driven away to Wimbledon police station, where I was formally charged with murder. The news swept round the estate. It was music to the ears of all those who'd pilloried me and it turned those who had merely held suspicions against me.

Down at the station I was allowed to call my solicitor. When he arrived his instructions were simple. Say nothing except, "No comment."

It was just as well. In the first of three interviews, DI Pedder gleefully revealed that Lizzie was, in reality, a police officer. I was shocked, as they intended, but I managed to keep quiet – even when they brought her in to confront and question me.

There was a mixture of anger, embarrassment and humiliation running through me. All those intimate thoughts and fantasies of mine had been pored over – and no doubt laughed at and

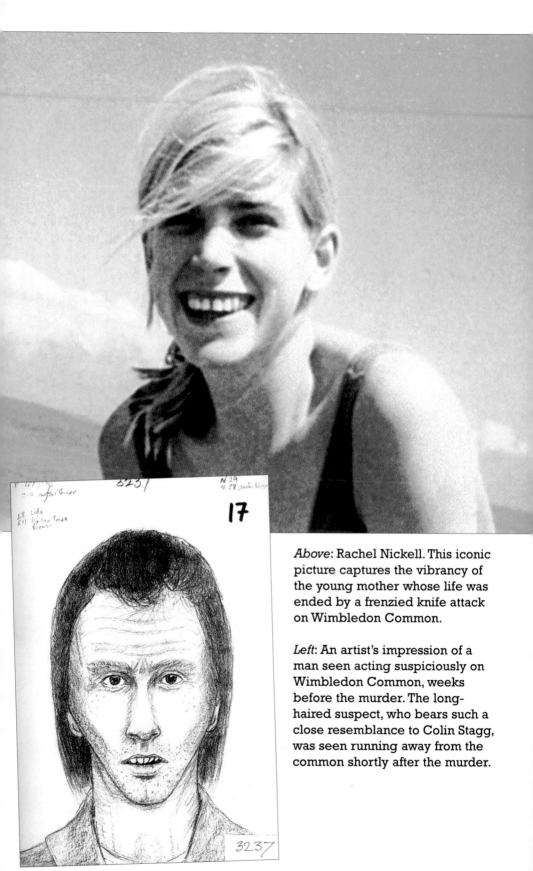

Above: Rachel Nickell. This iconic picture captures the vibrancy of the young mother whose life was ended by a frenzied knife attack on Wimbledon Common.

Left: An artist's impression of a man seen acting suspiciously on Wimbledon Common, weeks before the murder. The long-haired suspect, who bears such a close resemblance to Colin Stagg, was seen running away from the common shortly after the murder.

Right: Colin and his dog Brandy, at home during the early nineties. A quiet, unassuming man leading an unremarkable life.

Above: Colin is reunited with Brandy at the kennels, after thirteen months held on remand. Diane Beddoes, later to become his wife, is pictured right.

Left: Colin with Brandy, pictured in his back garden during the summer of 1993 – the year after the Nickell murder.

Above: Colin and Diane Stagg share a stress-free moment in a Shropshire cottage during filming of *The Cook Report*.

Right: Colin and Diane on their wedding day in August 1995, pictured with Lee Ashley.

Left: Colin and Diane Stagg celebrate their wedding with family members.

Right: Diane and Colin enjoy a boozy night in at the Shropshire cottage during filming of *The Cook Report*.

Above: Colin at the computer in his living room, displaying his stylised stag tattoo.

Right: Colin and his co-author, Ted Hynds, in the stocks at Nottingham Castle during a break in filming for *The Cook Report* in December 1996.

Below left: Former Detective Inspector Keith Pedder, who led the honeytrap undercover operation designed to extract a confession from Colin Stagg.

Below right: Paul Britton, the clinical psychologist and profiler who planned the flawed honeytrap operation. His tactics were savaged by Mr Justice Ognall at the Old Bailey.

Above left: Professor David Canter pioneered offender profiling in the UK and was the inspiration for the TV series *Cracker*. He was highly critical of Britton's handling of the covert operation.

Above right: Alex Tribick, the Staines solicitor who won Colin Stagg an ex gratia award from the Home Office, for being forced to live life as 'the man who got away with murder'.

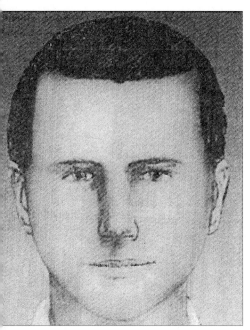

Below left: A photofit shown on BBC1's *Crimewatch* of the suspect seen by a witness shortly before the murder.

Below right: Robert Napper, a convicted double murderer and rapist held in Broadmoor, has become the new prime suspect in the Nickell case. Minute traces of DNA matching his own have been discovered on Rachel's underwear.

Above: On Wimbledon Common, standing beside an area map which shows the Windmill car park. Rachel Nickell left her vehicle there, just a few hundred yards from where she died.

Below left: Colin pictured on Wimbledon Common in 2002. He is standing close to the murder scene.

Below right: Colin with his latest pet Labrador, Jesse, outside their Roehampton home.

Colin, Jesse, and new girlfriend Terri.

Below: Colin pictured recently at home with Lee Ashley.

Colin with Terri
Marchant, with whom
he enjoys quiet
periods of domestic
bliss at her home in
Farnham.

ridiculed – by her and a team of detectives. (At that stage I was unaware of puppet-master Britton.)

There was an air of euphoria in the nick. A year's work on the country's highest profile murder case seemed to have paid off. The deputy assistant commissioner arrived to add his plaudits.

The old Gods must have laughed. But right then, I wasn't laughing. I was near to tears. They kept me overnight in the cells, ready for my appearance at the nearby magistrates' court next day.

My solicitor had warned me that, because of the seriousness of the charge, it could be nine months or even a year before I came to trial. And I was unlikely to be granted bail. That terrified me. The thought of being banged up, away from my home and from Brandy for so long, was frightening. I don't think I even considered what would happen if I was found guilty. I was in panic.

The hearing itself was a formality. The charge was read out, bail refused, and I was quickly remanded in custody to Wandsworth Prison. I was led in handcuffs to the prison van. As it reversed out of the back entrance to the court, it was mobbed by a crowd of reporters, photographers, TV cameramen and onlookers, some of whom had brought eggs to throw at the 'sex killer'.

What I didn't know was that four newspapers had broken the story of the undercover 'sting' that very morning. It was proof that detectives were tipping off the press. Pedder and his bosses were incandescent. Not only did they have a 'grass' – who a high-level inquiry would fail to trace – but they feared it might jeopardise the Lizzie James evidence.

I didn't know and I wouldn't have cared. I had to face my own problems as the massive prison gates clanged shut behind the van, and I faced my first night as a jailbird. It was to be another thirteen months before I tasted freedom again.

EIGHT

You think about women a lot inside – if you're 'normal' that is. Even behind bars, PG2656 Stagg was still a red-blooded Englishman. Despite the humiliation I'd suffered over Lizzie, women helped to make my stretch almost bearable.

The kindness of three ladies saved my sanity. Their letters helped keep my depression at bay. For, despite the brave face I always put on for prison staff and other cons, being locked up was a torment. All my life I had loved the outdoors. My daily walks across the common with my dog were my lifeblood. Being banged up in a cramped cell for twenty-three hours a day, I felt like a caged bird

My imagination worked against me. The stories I had heard about sex offenders being assaulted, raped or even worse took on a terrible significance. I knew what happened to nonces and it wasn't pretty. I adopted a sort of cheeky, nonchalant disposition, in the hope that my fellow cons would think I was too daft to have done something so terrible.

Keeping up this daily façade in front of other people was a terrible strain. Yet spending so much time alone with my imagined fears was equally traumatic. I dare not tell the doctor how I felt or I'd have been on suicide watch, tranquilisers or other drugs, which I hate. It would also have looked like a guilty conscience at work. I couldn't have that.

So I put on a show to convince the inmates everything was cool. But in my head I was hurting and fearful. That's why those letters became a lifeline to some sort of normality.

Prison is a frightening place. It terrified me *then* and the thought of it still does *now*. Over the months I calmed down a lot, but I never lost my fear. Bad things can happen there at any moment, and I never let my guard down. There's always a sense of danger. Not surprising when you're graded Cat A – 'highly dangerous' – and you're only a skinny five foot seven bloke who wouldn't hurt an ant!

But strangely, Lizzie's honeytrap may have helped me. Those newspaper stories about the covert operation had been read with mixed reactions by the cons. Some of them still thought I was the killer, but others were convinced I had been fitted up by a sneaky police operation. I can't say for certain, but my time inside could have been a lot worse.

After my release, I read a story that some of the toughest inmates had held a sort of kangaroo court to decide what to do with me when they heard I'd been charged and was coming to Wandsworth. The majority view was that I was the innocent victim of a set-up and should be left alone. But I didn't know that at the time, and I felt I had every reason to be very afraid.

Going through the dehumanising prison induction process seemed bad enough. Stripping for a shower, then dressing in the remand uniform of brown jeans and T-shirt, then being given a cursory medical. The doctor informed me I would initially be held in the hospital wing for assessment and my own safety. That last bit confirmed my fears.

Two warders escorted me to my cell, the only one designated Cat A on the wing, with an additional iron cage fitted over the door. Inside, it was bigger than I expected, but the sight of a bucket in the corner for my personal 'slops' was an odorous reminder of my status on a segregated wing. It hadn't been emptied by the previous occupant.

I missed my dog and was worried sick about what had happened to him. He had been left behind with the police who were searching my flat, and taken off to Battersea Dogs Home. Sitting on my creaky iron bed in this grim dungeon, a wave of loneliness and despair caught up with me. For someone who had never spent more than a few nights away from home in his life, it was a miserable experience with no immediate end in sight.

At the very least, I was looking at six months banged up before the committal went to court. If, as was likely, the magistrate sent me for trial at the Old Bailey, it would be over a year.

The question was whether I could survive when I was moved into the general prison population, even on a segregated wing. I was given a worrying indication later that day, after a welcome visit from my brother Lee and his wife Carol. As I was escorted back to my cell one of the inmates hissed, "Hanging's too good for him."

The guards rushed me back to my cell and left me to consider my possible fate. I was brought out again for an evening meal. But the food was awful and I could barely manage a bite.

Back in my cell I thought of Brandy and how he must be missing me. I hoped he was being cared for properly. I hardly slept that first night and was wide awake when the 6.30am klaxon sounded the start of the prison day.

It was to be my first full day with the other inmates, and I was very nervous as I joined the queue to empty my stinking slop bucket. I needn't have worried. Nobody took any notice of me. (Deliberately, I think.) But that didn't mean there was no violence to come.

Some days later, I had my first taste of how tempers can flare inside. It went off so suddenly. I was sat down watching two inmates playing pool. One of them took exception to this and growled, "Why don't you watch the TV?"

Trying to be clever, I stupidly replied, "I prefer to watch you two." With that he strode towards me, brandishing the cue. He scared the life out of me, but the adrenaline rush saved me. I jumped up, grabbed my chair and swung it at his head. I missed him by a fraction and, before he could retaliate, two officers moved in fast and hustled me back to my cell

On the way we passed one old lag who muttered, "I hope you die, you bastard." Things looked ugly and it seemed my worst fears were being realised. The screws were aggressive too, when I made attempts at jokey humour with them.

Then things got really scary. My mother turned up for a visit with Dave Carr, her husband. I had last seen them at my dad's funeral, seven years earlier, and not for years before that. She was effectively dead to me for what she had done to my dad and her family. But, considering my situation, it's perhaps not surprising that I was pleased to see what passed for friendly faces, even if they both looked glum.

I naïvely thought 'mother love' had proved too strong to ignore me in my time of need. I was grateful to see them both, even though I felt on edge.

I must have needed my head examined. The penny should have dropped when they immediately started complaining about press intrusion – as if it was my fault. Dave was banging on about "reporters swarming round our home like vultures, wanting information on you."

Even then it didn't click. I told them, "Don't blame me. You know nothing about me – either of you – so you've got nothing to tell them." I should have said 'sell them'. Looking pointedly at my mother, I added, "You weren't around most of the time I was growing up, and you haven't had anything to do with me since." She didn't say a word. Dave looked embarrassed and soon said it was time to go, but promised they would come back to see me again. I felt a bit mean at my reaction, so I thanked them for coming.

It never crossed my mind that they – and almost every other member of my family – were doing deals with newspapers. They were selling stories and photographs of me as fast, and for as much, as they could. So much for family solidarity. They were only interested in the money, but I didn't find that out – to my personal cost – until much later. My mother continued to visit, and I never suspected she had the ulterior motive of making money from the papers.

It was during my early days on the hospital wing that I started to receive letters from four other female 'fans', three of whom helped to ease my miserable time behind bars. The odd one out called herself Sandy Stevens, and her first letter arrived only a few days into my remand. She claimed to have once been raped by a man holding a knife, and that she found me exciting!

Fresh from the Lizzie James fiasco, I wasn't even tempted by her bizarre story or her claim to be falling for me. She sent me drawings which looked like Rachel, but which she said were intended as self-portraits. I immediately sensed another police trap and informed my solicitor. I had been here before. He understandably took the view that no rape victim could possibly be attracted to a potential knife killer, and advised me to ignore her. She continued writing for some while, but I blanked her letters. In her last one she vowed "undying love" for me. That was too close to Lizzie's line for comfort.

But about the same time, I received the first letter from a free-spirited brunette called Diane Beddoes, nee Rooney. She sounded genuine. A care worker from Milton Keynes, she believed I had been tricked by the police and promised her support. It turned out she was bisexual, with a healthy, no-nonsense approach to sex and, like me, loved nature, animals, and wanted a happy home.

After Lizzie's weirdness she was a breath of fresh air. I told her I was very open-minded when it came to sex, but I wasn't into anything weird! I drew strength by confiding my fears to her, and we began to correspond regularly. She was to play an important role in my life.

To be fair to her, she did admit from the start that she had had a drink problem, but I ignored this warning. (Another big mistake. A more appropriate maiden name for her might have been Looney, rather than Rooney.) So when Diane started writing to me in jail, I was delighted. She did send me some sex letters, and I replied in kind, but it was really tame stuff – a sort of verbal security blanket to fend off the misery of imprisonment.

Another lovely surprise was a letter from Lynda, the neighbour I had been hoping to start an affair with the day I was arrested and charged. It raised my spirits because she told me she was convinced of my innocence, and ended the note by saying, "I miss you and I want to fuck you more and more."

So not every woman thought I was a monster, and it seemed I was onto a promise. I only wish I had kept her to it later, instead of switching my affections.

Two months later, I was moved from the hospital wing and allowed open visits. Soon afterwards, one of the screws told me I had a visitor. To my surprise, my stepfather, Dave Carr, had brought Lynda to see me. It was brilliant – I couldn't thank him enough.

We met in the general visitor's room, and I was able to hug and kiss her. Having an attractive woman in my arms did a lot for my morale and drew a lot of envious looks from other prisoners. Lynda came to visit me a few times over the next year and wrote loving and supportive letters. She said she had fallen a little bit in love with me, but sadly, at the same time, I was falling for Diane.

(Neither of them knew about the other, and it caused me a bit of embarrassment when I was released. Diane moved in with me, and we were out walking the dog when we bumped into Lynda. I went over to speak to her. Surprisingly, Lynda was very laidback about things. She had read of my love for Diane in the papers and realised she'd lost out. There was no jealousy or recrimination on her part, and she was kind enough to say we would still be friends. She was a proper lady. But I had to pass her off as just a neighbour, as Diane had a jealous streak a mile wide and would have gone crazy.)

There was one other letter writer who proved to be the best of them all. She didn't profess undying love for me, talk dirty or want to bed me. She just wanted me to know she believed in my innocence.

Lee Ashley was a rather refined lady who lived at the top of a tower block a few hundred yards behind my back garden. We had seen each other around the estate for years; I knew her to nod a 'hello' to, but we'd never had a proper conversation. She was in her early fifties, always smartly dressed, and had worked with a lot of showbiz people in the past, so she wasn't easily impressed by fame (or infamy).

This was no publicity-hunting groupie. Lee was a highly intelligent woman who decided to take up my cause, having formed the view that the "quiet, polite young man" she was on nodding acquaintance with could not be a sadistic murderer. She decided to test her conviction by exchanging letters with me, quickly becoming convinced of the wrongness of my arrest, and has remained my staunchest friend and confidante ever since.

Perhaps it was because she was a more mature woman that I could admit my innermost fears to her without feeling self-conscious. But, like Lynda and Diane, I didn't tell her I was writing to other women. I wanted her to think she was the only one because I didn't want to risk losing her.

(I realised afterwards that it wouldn't have mattered to her. In any case she soon suspected, because I often asked her to send me more stamps!)

Lee has proved my rock. She has been there for me in all the bad times down the troubled years since I got out. She comforted me and helped me deal with the emotional wreckage of my marriage, and to come to terms with being an outcast. Back then, her calming, chatty jail-time letters helped me fight the depression that might otherwise have overwhelmed me. I owe her a debt that can never be repaid.

Despite these morale boosters, the claustrophobic atmosphere often got to me. A lot of the time I was banged up for twenty-three hours at a stretch. Though having always been a solitary person – one nickname as a kid was 'Monk', because I was always reading by myself – sometimes helped.

I tried to think of the cell as my bedroom, and shut out the noise and smell of so many bodies crammed in together. I've always been fussy, almost fastidious, about personal hygiene, and I hate bad smells. In Wandsworth I was never far from the unappetising tang of slops and disinfectant.

Other times, I felt so low I even refused the offer of an hour outside in the exercise yard and just lay there on my bed, letting waves of self-pity wash over me. After living poor but free for so long, I hated becoming institutionalised. I still think it was a small miracle that I didn't lose my mind during those thirteen long months. Luckily, relations with my fellow inmates weren't too bad.

I did get punched in the face once, but the only really bad incident was being scalded. Before remand prisoners get locked in for the night, hot water is delivered to their cells so they can make tea. The hot-water urn is pulled by a prisoner. On this night, as I held out my mug, he deliberately moved the boiling water tap over my hand. I screamed in agony as my hand blistered up, but I didn't report it. Neither did the female officer who watched it happen. I thought the authorities would dismiss it as an 'accident', and the cons would regard me a wimp, or worse – a grass.

By and large, the officers treated me reasonably well. One even gave me two cigarettes, when I chanced my luck in the exercise yard and asked if he had a fag to spare. But there were a couple of them who were real nasty bastards. They would patrol up to my cell each night, open the spyhole and make remarks like, "Why doesn't this cunt hang himself?" This was often followed by, "If he doesn't, we can always do it for him. Nobody would know." It was designed to terrify, and it scared the shit out of me.

Inmates would have to rely on chance to get me, because I was only allowed one hour for association each day for the first nine months. The officers had the run of the prison. They could plan their move and get me any time they chose. But their sick 'comedy' routine ended when I became so scared that I complained to the governor. I never heard from them again.

The only relief from the prison regime was my monthly visits to the magistrates' court, where every bail plea was rejected and I was remanded back to Wandsworth for another month. Christmas came and went without any cheer for me. The committal was approaching, and I had no confidence that the case would be thrown out. I was sure to face an Old Bailey judge in another six or seven months. And so it proved.

My legal team had opted for an 'old-style' hearing which contained a mixture of live evidence and statements. Their idea was to test the prosecution evidence and witnesses, and then present the argument to stipendiary magistrate Terry English that there was no case for me to answer.

The hearing opened on February 17th 1994, and played to a packed house for eleven days. The press were going frantic because reporting restrictions were not lifted, so they couldn't write about the evidence. Not that they were much interested in the circumstantial evidence of Jane Harriman, Susan Gale or Lillian Avid.

They didn't want to know about whether I was the suspect seen on or near the common – or even whether I was the murderer, as according to a daft old woman. What had them drooling was the prospect of a blonde sexpot policewoman describing in detail how she swapped pornographic fantasies with a suspected killer.

They were to be disappointed. She gave a brief, thirty-minute testimony shielded by a wooden screen and was only visible to me, the magistrate and the barristers. At one point my counsel, Jim Sturman, suggested, "You were trying to find out if he would incriminate himself in the murder of Rachel Nickell."

She dismissed the idea. "No. I was trying to find out if he was implicated or not." That sounded very much like the same thing to me. Then I cringed when she revealed that her porno tape recording – which had turned me on so much – had been put together by Keith Pedder and Mike Wickerson, under guidance of Paul Britton. Lizzie had been speaking in her master's voice, and I felt sick with embarrassment. I'd been given a hard-on by a couple of fellers. I prayed the cons never found out.

My team tried to have her evidence and Britton's thrown out. Mr Sturman said his evidence was essentially, "I am Britton, therefore I am right. There is no scientific analysis to explain his conclusions." The evidence, he added, was "speculative and unsupported by anything other than Mr Britton's own intuition. This type of witness could be a dangerous type of animal."

He said Lizzie's letters were 'come-ons' contrived to get me to put my "wildest fantasies on paper. You would have had to be a moron not to know this was a woman who wanted to be dominated. No wonder Mr Stagg replied in the way he did."

On the last day Mr Sturman argued valiantly to have the case thrown out, describing Britton's evidence as contradictory and Lizzie as "raising the ante" to get me to confess. But prosecutor Bill Boyce said that a jury should have the chance to hear all the evidence, and then to "make up their minds whether Colin Stagg was a murderer or a victim of his own fantasies."

I thought that was a bit rich. I only made up those fantasies in response to Lizzie's opening letter, which gave the impression she was deeply into extreme sex. Frankly, it was a struggle sometimes, to keep up with her demands for more and more weird and dangerous themes.

At that time I had a very limited practical knowledge of sex, and she kept leading me into deeper and darker places. I went along with her demands because, after meeting her, I fancied her even more. But I wasn't always comfortable at what she was suggesting. In fact, I really thought she was a bit mad.

The magistrate, however, took the path of least resistance and sent me for trial, leaving it up to the judge and jury to decide my fate. Bail was once more refused.

For weeks afterwards I was in a black mood. The months before my trial stretched ahead of me like an eternity. And the injustice of being locked up with a bunch of real criminals gnawed at me. Day after day these thoughts festered inside. And I became more fearful for my safety.

Then, in early spring, came some news that dramatically raised my hopes. Up north, at Leeds Crown Court, a police undercover operation very similar to Lizzie's had come spectacularly unstuck. A grocer called Keith Hall from Pudsey had been charged with murdering his wife. As with me, the police had made him the prime suspect but could find no evidence.

His wife had vanished without trace the day after neighbours heard a blazing row between them. Then he answered a lonely hearts ad, only a few months after he claimed his wife had walked out on him. This woman, like Julie Pines, became suspicious and contacted the police. They seized the chance to get an undercover policewoman to adopt her identity.

Incredibly, the name she used was 'Liz', and they had a series of letters, phone calls and meetings over five months. The breakthrough came when he asked her to marry him, because he said his wife wasn't ever coming back. That was enough for them to arrest and charge him.

After days of legal argument, the judge ruled that the months of undercover evidence – including Hall's taped assertion about his wife – were inadmissible. Hall walked free without going before a jury. It was a real morale boost for me. But, although my legal team were encouraged, they warned me that the judge's ruling in Leeds was not a binding precedent. The judge in my own trial could choose to ignore it. That dampened my good mood. I had hoped the judgement would lead to my early release, but they told me there was no hope of that. I still had to go to trial.

My dreary, mind-numbing existence continued. The only slice of luck was when Diane managed to get a visit, even though she wasn't on the official visitors' list. I thought she was really nice looking, full of life. My only worry was that she might be disappointed with me. But she wasn't.

In the meantime, my defence had arranged psychological tests.

Dr Gisli Gudjonsson put me through a wide series of scientifically recognised personality and sexuality tests. The conclusion revealed "no evidence of mental illness, personality disorder, or sexual deviancy." (I could have told them that!) A far more telling report came from Glen Wilson at the Institute of Psychiatry. He wrote:

Stagg's fantasies are revealed in his letters to Julie Pines, Lizzie James and Janet George.

But a distinction needs to be made between those freely generated, and hence truly representative of his preferences, and those evoked by Lizzie James.

Over a long period of communication she shapes fantasies which bear similarity to the Rachel Nickell murder. In my opinion, the latter give no reliable guide as to the true sexual preferences of Mr Stagg . . .

The fantasies that appear spontaneously produced by Stagg include a number of themes such as outdoor sex, reference to nature, grass, and trees, the risk of exposure/discovery, being seen, watched, stumbled across by strangers in the woods, voyeurism, watching or spying on others, incorporating passers-by into masturbation ceremonies, oral sex, rear entry, group sex activity, genital descriptions and manifestations of orgasm.

None of these is particularly abnormal.

They are understandable in relation to his self-admitted level of sexual experience and maturity, his social isolation, and his life-style of walking a dog on Wimbledon Common and sometimes nude sunbathing there.

The manner in which these fantasies are expressed might appear crude, but is typical of the content of male fantasies and consistent with the material found in men's magazines such as Escort and Fiesta.

On his own report Stagg is an isolated and sexually inexperienced individual and would therefore be dependent on pornography and fantasies.

Men fantasize most when deprived and frustrated. While Stagg does appear to have an active fantasy life it is not exceptional for a young man without access to actual partners.

Stagg's propensity to write out his fantasies is also not uncommon, as evidenced by the steady stream of letters to magazines such as Forum, *and is probably related to his introversion and awkwardness in conversation, even on the telephone. His spontaneously given fantasies are not especially deviant.*

Then he made a telling point:

Stagg does ultimately produce some more bizarre sexual fantasies, including threats with a knife, blood-letting and blood-drinking.

But there is a distinct likelihood that these were produced in order to please and excite Lizzie James. In fact he was subjected over a long period of time to a process of prompting and selective reinforcement known as operant conditioning − popularly called brainwashing . . .

Given Stagg's mounting frustration, having worked months to seduce Lizzie, it is perhaps surprising that he did not ultimately claim to be 'that man'.

Such a confession, had it occurred, would be worthless.

The fact that he produced a false confession, to a crime that never happened, upon a prescription of Lizzie James is evidence that the deviant fantasies, ultimately evoked from him, were probably also tailored to excite her, rather than as expressions of his own deviant desire . . .

I do not find the profile of sexual fantasies exhibited by Stagg is either unique or deviant.

A high proportion of respectable men within the general population use fantasies to enhance their sexual arousal which have elements of voyeurism, group sex, sex with strangers, sex in public places and sadomasochism, which might appear perverted if acted upon.

In the case of Stagg we cannot even have confidence that his more bizarre and crime-related fantasies were really his own and not suggested by Lizzie James − indeed the latter is more likely.

It is therefore my opinion that the attempt to link Stagg's fantasies with a fantasy profile, hypothesized to characterise the murderer of Rachel Nickell, is unsatisfactory.

That made it clear then. I'd been subjected to a form of brainwashing. But would the jury dismiss this as merely a disagreement of experts over one part of the case?

As my trial date approached my lawyers obviously needed more contact with me, so it seemed very suspicious when I was suddenly moved to Winchester jail at the end of June. This was a much softer place, which seemed strange for a Cat A prisoner like me. It seemed like I'd been moved to make it more awkward for my legal team to reach me. So, although I enjoyed the laidback regime, they had me back in Wandsworth within a fortnight. I regarded my stay in Hants as a holiday break.

The trial was set for Monday September 5th and, as the day approached, so my fears increased. Despite the Keith Hall judgement and the flimsy circumstantial nature of the evidence against me, things could still go wrong. Juries are only human and can be swayed by emotion in the face of a lack of hard evidence. Rachel's murder had caused a lot of strong emotions.

I wore a brand new long-sleeved shirt, one of three sent by Lee Ashley, for my first appearance at the Bailey. It was one of the few I had ever owned, and she wanted me to look smarter than in my usual T-shirt outfit.

The hearing didn't last much more than half an hour. The judge decided he needed three days to familiarise himself with the seven hundred-odd pages relating to Operation Edzell, and adjourned for three days. After that, he would hear the legal arguments over the undercover operation and make his ruling as to what was admissible evidence.

When we all returned on Thursday, my counsel, Bill Clegg

QC, opened the defence. He and prosecutor John Nutting went on until Monday afternoon. When they had finished the judge said he would announce his decision on Wednesday the 14th.

Those two days seemed the longest of my life. It had become clear that my fate rested on the admissibility of Lizzie's evidence. If it was allowed then in all probability I would be found guilty.

NINE

I needn't have worried.

Mr Justice Ognall took forty-five minutes to fillet the prosecution case. It was a lengthy judgement and a ferocious one. He methodically demolished the so-called evidence of the undercover operation and described it as a "gross deception".

I had entered the dock with my guts churning – either from nerves or the prison breakfast. My life was in the hands of this stern, red-robed figure. I hadn't a clue what he was going to say. But I doubted that, if he allowed Lizzie's evidence, the jury would see how flimsy and manipulative it all was. They might interpret my sex fantasies like Britton did, and bang me up for life.

But the judge began by briefly outlining the background to my arrest and charge, including my sex fantasy letter to JP (Julie Pines). Then he cut straight to the heart of the profiling operation:

"The circumstances of the killing of Rachel Nickell were peculiarly brutal and suggested that the murderer was sexually deviant.

"In an effort to identify that man the police had enlisted the services of a clinical psychologist, Mr Paul Britton.

"Using the evidence in the possession of the police at that time, as to the nature and general circumstances surrounding the killing, Mr Britton prepared a profile of the type of person he would expect the offender to be.

"It was his opinion that the murderer would fall within a particularly small sub-class of male sexual deviants who would, in his opinion, betray a number of relatively peculiar characteristics or sexual idiosyncrasies.

"In particular, it was his opinion that, given the appropriate opportunity and time, the murderer would be disposed to indulge in very special and extreme sexual fantasies, and that ultimately the revelation of those fantasies, would in turn lead him to discuss and finally confess to the murder.

"Nobody questions that in certain cases the assistance of a psychologist of that kind can prove a very useful investigative tool. But in this case the police went much further.

"In constant consultation with Mr Britton they set up an undercover operation. It lasted some seven months. It took this form: A woman police officer, known for the purposes of this operation as Lizzie James, was to introduce herself to the accused as a friend of JP, who had seen his, the accused's, letters to that lady and who, unlike JP, would express herself as being intrigued and stimulated by their sexual content.

"Thereafter the relationship was to be allowed to develop in writing, by telephone and by meetings – all this under the constant supervision and direction of the psychologist."

As he continued in his calmly methodical way, my confidence suddenly began to soar. He was starting to rubbish Britton's theories.

"It was hoped that within the development of that liaison there would or might be betrayed first fantasies of the kind described by Mr Britton, and ultimately in line with his prognosis, an admission of guilt.

"I have been told Mr Britton was of the opinion that the ultimate extreme fantasies – and indeed the consequent confession of guilt – would be likely to follow within a time bracket as short as two weeks from the inception of the liaison and, at the latest, within sixteen weeks of its commencement.

"In fact, as will be apparent, the relationship lasted nigh on twenty-eight weeks, of which it is common ground only the last twelve weeks or so are said, for the Crown's purposes, to have been probatively productive.

"I should say at once that the prosecution sought to persuade me that the object of the exercise was to afford the accused the opportunity either to eliminate himself from the inquiry or implicate himself in the murder.

"I am bound to say I regard that description of the operation as highly disingenuous."

I homed in on those last two words. They seemed like legalese for 'total bollocks'! Was he going to savage the whole sting operation? Hope grew steadily as he spoke.

"It is very important to my mind to note that at no stage during this very protracted operation did the accused ever admit that he was the murderer. Indeed, to the contrary, he repeatedly denied it.

"Even when latterly and as part of the plan he was invited by Lizzie James to admit the crime, as a condition of continuing a liaison that he was manifestly desperate to maintain at almost all cost, he continued to say that he was innocent of this offence.

"Moreover it should be noted that in two very material respects, in describing the nature of the killing as he understood it, in his exchanges with Lizzie James, this accused got it wrong.

"He mis-described the precise locus of the body in the wood on Wimbledon Common and he said that the victim had been raped; she had not."

Referring to my seven-month relationship with Lizzie, he added, "Despite his repeated denials as to being the murderer, it is apparent from the transcripts that during a substantial period of time the accused wrote numerous letters to Lizzie James in which he fantasised in an explicit and progressively more extreme fashion about sexual matters.

"Mr Britton – if I may be forgiven for using the phrase – was pulling the strings and, as the operation went on, he compared the totality of Stagg's outpourings with the profile of the murderer that he had constructed as part of the initial police investigation.

"It was his opinion, at the end of it all, that there was a precise overlap between his profile of the killer and the man the accused revealed himself to be in the fantasies expressed to Lizzie James.

"Thus in effect, it would be his opinion that, on that material and based upon that comparison and conclusion, the accused was identified as the murderer of Rachel Nickell.

"I need, I hope, only to recite the effect of that evidence for its novelty as admissible evidence in a criminal trial to be recognised.

"I am not at all surprised that there is no authority in any common law – or what I shall call quasi-common law jurisdiction – to the effect that such evidence has ever been treated as properly admissible in proof of identity."

He added later: "When first interrogated this accused revealed to the police that he was a desperately lonely man and a sexual virgin, and a man who longed for a long-term sexual liaison with a woman.

"I am satisfied that from the inception of the operation Lizzie James, no doubt under instruction, played upon that loneliness and those aspirations.

"Although I have been referred to very many pages of transcript by Mr Clegg, it is only necessary to refer to some of them for present purposes.

"I preface those references by this observation. In common sense the exercise would only achieve its purpose if the accused ultimately betrayed the full nature of his fantasies as forecast by Mr Britton, for otherwise that psychologist could not undertake the necessary matching exercise.

"It is common ground before me that, from mid-January 1993 until mid-May, nothing had emerged from the accused to support Mr Britton's ultimate diagnosis.

"What was the conduct of Lizzie James, as instructed, which led to that turning point in time?

"Although Mr Nutting characterises the accused's responses as progressive and voluntary, I do not think that is borne out by a careful study of the material.

"The increasingly extreme character of the fantasies was the product of deliberate shaping by the policewoman and encouragement by her.

"Much of what she said to him demands the conclusion that she was deliberately deceiving the accused by encouraging him to express his innermost fantasies because she enjoyed them, and the more extreme the better.

"Using the test of whether or not the suspect was tricked or voluntarily applied himself to the trick, it is perhaps relevant to note that this whole liaison begins with a letter written by Lizzie James, which clearly hints both at sexual deviancy and the prospect of a long term relationship with the suspect.

"By mid-February the accused had written two fantasy letters, but of course neither began to correspond with the profile proffered by the psychologist.

"They are, I suppose, fantasies not infrequently in the minds of lonely, heterosexual young men, though perhaps rarely expressed . . .

"The lengths to which this man was being manipulated are evidenced by the fact that, by the middle of May ten weeks or so later, he was prepared to confess to a murder which he said he perpetrated at the age of thirteen in the New Forest, which crime in fact never occurred at all and which confession was plainly prompted in a desperate effort to preserve his relationship with Lizzie James . . .

"It is to my mind not irrelevant to note that even up to that stage, the accused was at pains expressly to deny that he was the Wimbledon murderer – and this despite obvious attempts to persuade him to admit directly that he was the killer.

"It reveals to my mind a persistent attempt by this officer to elicit a confession, without which she is saying their relationship can come to nothing; it fails.

"It serves to demonstrate, it seems to me, lengths to which the police were prepared to go in this operation.

"This was no doubt prompted by the fact that the sixteen-week maximum period predicted by Mr Britton had now expired without bearing any probative fruit.

"To suggest that by this time the exercise was as much exculpatory as inculpatory, does not bear examination."

Referring to Lizzie's own sex tape, he said, "Perhaps the most vivid illustration of what is described as the shaping of the accused's mind and feelings is to be found in mid-June of 1993, five months into the relationship.

"The accused had by now started to reveal fantasies of potential significance to the psychologist. On or about 16th June Lizzie James dictated onto a cassette a fantasy which she sent to the accused.

"It is a highly explicit document or tape. It contains references to male domination, group sex, the use of a knife by a man to heighten sexual excitement.

"It is scarcely surprising that thereafter, both in writing and orally, the accused continues to speak of a knife in the context of a sexual encounter.

"Mr Clegg did not pull his punches in this regard. He submitted that for a serving police officer to prepare and dispatch this tape was disgraceful conduct.

"It was certainly thoroughly reprehensible.

"I must bear in mind of course that the policewoman was acting under orders and that the police in their turn were being guided by the psychologist. But that cannot excuse their instigation of this sort of stratagem.

"I would be the first to acknowledge the very great pressures on the police in their pursuit of this grave enquiry, but I am afraid that this behaviour betrays not merely an excess of zeal but a substantial attempt to incriminate a suspect by positive and deceptive conduct of the grossest kind."

By now my heart was hammering, although I tried to keep the smile off my face. After that knockout punch, he couldn't possibly allow the evidence. His next words confirmed it.

"A careful appraisal of all the material demonstrates a skilful and sustained enterprise to manipulate the accused. Sometimes subtle, sometimes blatant in its technique.

"It was designed by deception to manoeuvre and seduce him to reveal fantasies of a suggested incriminating character, and additionally, and as it turned out, wholly unsuccessfully, to admit the offence.

"I believe that the defence are correct to describe this operation as misconceived. The prosecution submitted to me that to test the accused's capacity to fantasise the undercover operation was 'the only route available'.

"So be it. But if that route involves clear trespass into the territory of impropriety, the court must stand firm and bar the way."

I almost couldn't dare believe it. *I was finally going home!*

There was just time for him to rub salt in the police's wounds. Referring to my last meeting with Lizzie in Hyde Park, the judge added, "She demonstrated that the accused had indicated that the victim's hands were palm to palm by her side as if in prayer.

"The prosecution submit that when the accused gave this demonstration of the position of the hands and arms, as re-demonstrated thereafter by Lizzie James, he could not have derived that knowledge from photograph ten of KP/27 which was the only photograph shown to him by the police.

"It is said that photograph fifteen of KP/27, which does illustrate the position of the hands, reveals that what Lizzie James says the accused demonstrated is in fact true and could only have therefore been known to him because he was the assailant.

"The prosecution submit that this piece of evidence amounts to a confession. But the hands of the victim were not palm-to-palm at all.

"The arms are in fact crossed at the wrist so that the hands barely touch.

"It is said by the defence that this is not a 'minor difference' as the Crown expressed it in argument, but a discrepancy which completely undermines the whole thesis, or if not completely, is so flimsy in its quality that its suggestive probative value is outweighed by its prejudicial effect."

So my insistence that Lizzie had lied about my demonstration was believed. And better yet, there was a swipe at Britton's profiling. Before booting Lizzie's evidence out of court, the judge added, "The notion that a psychological profile is in any circumstances admissible in proof of identity is to my mind redolent with considerable danger.

"First because of the rule against evidence going solely to propensity; second because the suggested analogy between this case and the authorities on so-called similar fact evidence is *prima facie* highly questionable.

"And third because of the question of whether this is truly described as expert evidence at all."

All that remained was for the judge to officially bar the Lizzie James material; the prosecution then offered no further evidence, and a formal verdict of Not Guilty was recorded.

With those two words I imagined my nightmare was over. Almost thirteen months to the day since my arrest, I was a free man again. Within an hour I was drinking champagne with my legal team, toasting their success and looking forward to a bright future.

There was a sexy woman waiting for me; a lucrative newspaper deal lined up; and a certain end to the hate campaign, now I had been found not guilty. To complete my revenge, the police and Paul Britton were to be taken to the cleaners in a costly civil action.

But I'd soon have the smile wiped off my face. The love of my life would turn into a greedy, money-grubbing drunk; I would be ripped off – first by my family, then by the papers; I would become the hate figure of a generation. My arch-enemies never got to court, while I became unemployable

Freedom was just another name for a life sentence. The euphoria of my release didn't last long, but still – I have to admit that, after Wandsworth Prison, anything would have felt like Heaven.

The first hint of what was about to happen to me came in a dignified, but embittered, statement read by Rachel's father, Andrew Nickell, outside the court. He made it quite clear how he viewed the judge's remarks, and how he viewed me:

"The pendulum has swung too far to the side of the criminal.

"Why has this situation arisen when society seems to care more for the criminal and less for the victim and their families? When is society and government going to redress the balance so that the scales of justice are level?"

After paying tribute to Lizzie James' 'bravery' for "putting her life on the line," he added, "At the end of the operation the police, the psychologist and the Crown Prosecution all had their own views as to whether Stagg was the murderer.

"Thirteen months later, having been committed for trial, Stagg now walks free. He has not been tried by a jury. His lordship, Mr Justice Ognall, ruled that the police undercover operation broke the rules laid down to ensure a safe conviction.

"The ruling is well argued in law and guided by many a precedent. The effect, however, is to rule that all the evidence gained during the undercover operation is inadmissible in a court of law. The law has been upheld, but where is the justice?"

He made a dramatic pause and went on. "I understand that the police will now keep the file on my daughter's murder open. They are not looking for anyone else!

"We have an impasse which may, and I emphasise *may*, put other daughters and wives at risk in the months and years ahead.

"The imbalance in the law allowed a defendant to stay silent during a trial without any significance being drawn to the fact.

"The whole evidence in this case, I believe ten thousand pages, is given to the defence for them to study and to find an answer.

"The prosecution have no appeal whatsoever against today's decision. If it was the other way round, then Colin Stagg's lawyers could have taken his case to the Court of Appeal.

"If the defence has the right of appeal, why not let the case be heard by a jury and not stifle the evidence? At every stage it seems the defendant has the advantage. We, as a society, require fairness for all, not just for the criminal."

His message was clear and simple. Colin Stagg was his daughter's murderer – who had got away with it on a technicality, thanks to a liberal-minded judge. The police and the psychologist did a great job, but were let down by the law. The trial should have gone ahead. After all, if I was found guilty I had the right to appeal.

His final twist of the knife came in saying that the police were not looking for anyone else. This was code for, "The police know he did it, but can't prove it." Those words registered, but I didn't pay them too much attention at the time. More importantly, I didn't expect anyone else to.

I may not have liked what he said, but I could sympathise with him. The poor man had lost his daughter in the most horrible circumstances – and then had what he saw as closure snatched away from him by the judge.

But I was too busy enjoying the air of freedom to worry about what the future held in store.

TEN

A rock hit my window, seconds after I'd left what I use as my study at the back of the flat. I heard the crash while I was in the toilet. There was a hole in the pane and glass on the floor, but no sign of the missile.

The police were called because our council won't repair any damage without a crime number. They sent detectives instead of uniforms, because they suspected it might have been a bullet! At any rate, they decided the hole was too big for a bullet and put it down to local 'hooliganism'. I found the piece of rock in the garden after they had gone.

That was my welcome back to the Alton estate in September 1994, after more than a year in prison, on remand for a crime I never committed. It wasn't to be the last such greeting. I'd suffered similar hate attacks and abuse in the months following my first arrest and release, three days later, in September 1992, with a 'prime suspect' tag effectively stuck to me.

But I'd naïvely expected the Not Guilty verdict to have put a stop to all that. It's ironic that the detective who opposed my bail at the committal hearing had justified it by warning something like this would happen. DI Pedder had told the magistrate, "The outrage caused by the murder is a threat to his personal safety. The estate is divided into two camps – those for Mr Stagg and those vehemently against him."

Prophetic words that still hold good today. Although DNA seems to have linked a double killer in Broadmoor to Rachel's murder, as long ago as 2004, he has yet to be prosecuted. And no apology to me has ever been forthcoming from the police. Of course, it avoids the humiliation of admitting the full extent of the damage caused to me, and to the Nickell murder inquiry, by their crackpot scheme.

It also blurs the grim fact that, by concentrating on me, they may have left her killer free to murder a mother and her little daughter fifteen months later. Britton went as far as insisting there was no possible link between the two crimes, and Pedder went along with him – despite the similarity of the frenzied stabbings.

The Met plainly hopes that the Nickell case will remain in limbo forever. As long as the Broadmoor inmate is not charged, they can justify not making a categorical declaration of my innocence. It also sends an obvious message to the public that I'm still connected to Rachel's murder. That message has echoed loudly down the years.

I've had to develop a hard shell to survive. The first three or four years were the worst. Whether I was indoors or out on the street there was always the risk of attack, both physical and verbal.

It gradually eased off, but the threat is still there even today. Over time, some of the people I grew up with moved off the estate, and new families came in who didn't know me. But it didn't take long for newcomers to learn about the monster in their midst. I've had kids who weren't born when Rachel died calling me 'murderer'.

Not so long ago, I overhead a couple having a real shouting match in the street outside. At one point, the bloke shouted, "If you don't shut up I'll get that Colin Stagg to do you!" I was a bit shocked, but not surprised. I'm the local bogeyman. Sometimes I can even laugh at the nonsense that is talked about me. Sometimes I challenge the name-callers, which shuts them up. But most of the time I ignore it.

Try to imagine what it would feel like to know that a lot of ordinary people still think you are a murderer, over thirteen years after your name should have been cleared. And all you can do is grin and bear it. But that's what can happen when the police get it wrong and won't own up.

All this was far from my thoughts on that first night of freedom, tucked up in the four-star Waldorf Hotel less than a mile from the Old Bailey. Watching the rain beating against my hotel window, I savoured the club sandwich from room service, raided the mini-bar and contemplated the difference that twenty-four hours had made to my life.

The contrast between my bleak cell and this luxury suite was mind-blowing. "I am not a number anymore!" I shouted in true *Prisoner* style, down at the empty Aldwych pavements. For the first time in a year I was no longer living on top of my toilet. There was none of that pungent prison smell of shit, sweat and dozens of male bodies crammed together.

Very soon, I'd be reunited with my dog for long walks on southwest London's greenspaces. Prison would be just a bad memory; I had a new girlfriend too, and there would be money in my pocket.

The whole day had become a blur. I had walked out of court

into a madhouse. Hundreds of onlookers, reporters, photographers and TV people were lying in wait, shouting questions, popping flash bulbs. They swarmed round, crowding me up against the Old Bailey wall. The TV lights almost blinded me as I struggled to read a short prepared statement.

It should have ended with the words, "I hope the police will now go out and find the real killer." But my anger and resentment took over and I made an unscripted addition – "the fat lazy bastards!"

Next moment I was hustled into a waiting taxi and driven away from court. My legal team took me back to their chambers in the Temple for a champagne celebration, as much for relief as victory. There were drinks and congratulations all round.

Even my mother's arrival didn't spoil the party. But she and Dave soon showed their true colours. It was always about money with them, as I should have realised sooner. They had done a deal to sell a reunion picture of me and my mother, plus my whole inside story, to a tabloid daily paper. Luckily my lawyer quickly put a stop to that, much to their obvious disappointment. He was already negotiating for big money on my behalf and wasn't going to let them cash in and spoil it.

He eventually agreed a £50,000 exclusive deal with the *News of the World*, who paid for my stay at the Waldorf, provided I passed a lie detector test. They allowed me to do a couple of short TV interviews so long as I didn't speak to newspapers. Joan Thirkettle, who had been convinced of my innocence, did the interview for ITN.

She asked the key question that everyone wanted to hear: "Did you kill Rachel Nickell?"

I replied firmly, "No, I did not. A crime like this is a crime against God, against the universe itself. I believe all life is sacred, from insects to human beings." Then I expressed my sympathy for the Nickell family. "I feel very sorry for them because they were seeing a man who was obviously set up by the police, when they should have been seeing the real murderer." For the local *BBC Newsroom South East*, I added this message for them: "Don't be angry with me. Be angry with the police who set me up and let the real murderer go free."

After those TV interviews, I left my newspaper minders and my legal team to celebrate in the bar while I went upstairs to my room. I wanted to be alone because I had something very important on my mind. I was going to get laid at last, as soon as I could get Diane to join me.

I phoned her number in Milton Keynes from the room, but her boyfriend said she was working. I left a message for her to call me at the hotel and settled down to enjoy the peaceful, luxurious surroundings while I waited.

It was late when she phoned back, but we chatted until five in the morning. It seemed like we had known each other all our lives. My solicitor and the *News of the World* minders were very suspicious of Diane. They thought she had got close to me in order to sell a story to someone else. But when I asked if she had a suggestion as to where I should sell, she replied, "I don't give a toss. All I want is to be with you." That was good enough for me.

I arranged for her to travel down to my counsel's chambers, so that one of his staff could escort her to where I was staying. It seemed that I would be moved the next morning because rival papers had discovered which hotel I was at.

After my first full English breakfast the journalists quickly drove me off to the Holiday Inn in west London, which was where my mother caught up with me – to my cost. She had managed to get a message passed on for me to phone her, which I stupidly did. She was harping on about journalists pestering her and Dave, so I explained that I had done a fifty grand deal with the 'News of the Screws' and that was the end of it. Of course, she immediately sold that information on to rival papers, and as a result I was screwed by the *News of the World*, who later deducted £9,000 from my fee! Thanks Mum.

But at the time my only thoughts centred on Diane, and what we would soon be doing on my big bed. When she was escorted to my room at last, carrying a big bottle of whisky, we fell into each other's arms. And that was all we did – kiss and cuddle – because of constant interruptions.

Eventually we lay on the bed and started to read the newspaper coverage about me. It was massive. I was front-page news everywhere, and it wasn't all good. It didn't seem to matter at the time. I'd foolishly expected that I'd now be finally vindicated. That didn't happen, but the sign of things to come didn't register with me. I was on too big a high.

'No Girl Is Safe' roared *The Sun*, between pictures of me and Rachel. Their story said the "mystery sex beast" who killed Rachel was now "laughing at the law amid fears he would kill again". The *Mirror* headline was 'Now I'll Make A Killing', a snide reference to the damages I hoped to get from the Met. I never said anything like that headline, but why let a little thing like that spoil the story? 'Where Is The Justice?' said the *Express*. The *Mail* followed a similar theme: its headline was 'The Child Who Still Waits For Justice', alongside a picture of Rachel and baby Alex.

Over the coming days, my mother's disclosure of my newspaper deal provoked fresh controversy, because the compensation payout to little Alex as a victim of serious crime was likely to be much less. 'It Stinks!' raged the *Daily Star*'s front-page editorial. Their article was typical of the way the press have always treated me, right up to the present day. Full of lies, half-truths, bile and spin. It read: "Why should a convicted flasher, a misfit who could not hold down a full-time job, a creature who lurked in a sordid flat plastered with satanic symbols and boasted in kinky letters of committing acts of self-abuse on Wimbledon Common . . . why should such a disgusting excuse for a man grow rich because he spent thirteen months in custody? Would he have put that time to better use? A quarter of a million pounds worth of better use?"

That one was deeply hurtful, but I still shrugged it off. It was just more sour grapes from the gutter press. Nobody, I convinced myself, was going to heed all that nonsense after I passed the *News of the World's* lie detector test. The paper had hired Jeremy Barratt, the country's leading polygraph expert, to administer it.

Funnily enough, when they took me to his home I discovered he lived only about a mile from Wimbledon Common. We had seen each other while walking our dogs. Like ITN, he asked the big question: "Did you kill Rachel Nickell?" "No," I replied firmly. "The needles on the polygraph didn't even flicker," trumpeted the paper. What the story didn't mention was that the test also cleared me of masturbating on the common – though it did announce that Diane had finally 'taken my cherry'. At the ripe old age of thirty-one, I was at last no longer a virgin!

By then we had been moved to yet another hotel, this time on top of Richmond Hill. We stayed there until after my story appeared on Sunday morning, then took a cab to my mother's place. We had no option. The council had put a security grill over my front door, to keep squatters out, and my daft brother Lee had lost the key.

When we arrived at Mum's place the press were waiting. She ushered us inside, and then brought in a journalist she had struck another deal with – for herself, of course. It was too much hassle to argue, so we gave him an interview and had our pictures taken. Later on we went for a walk, and endured our first experience of what life was going to be like.

We popped into a packed lunchtime pub, but before I could buy a drink this load voice bellowed: "You're going to get yours, you fucking murderer!" We left in a hurry. Diane was furious. She wanted to stick one on him – and she was big enough to do so. But I wanted to avoid trouble, so we left.

I could tell it had shaken her, so I said it was only because of the newspaper stories. People would soon forget about me. After that we just wanted to get home. I think my mother was glad to see us go, so Dave borrowed some bolt cutters and drove us back to my flat.

After a lot of trouble we managed to break through the grill and get inside. Home at last! But there was nothing sweet about it. The place was shambles. The police search teams had pulled my things apart and then left, without tidying up. It was dank and dismal.

We couldn't sleep on the bed because the only mattress had been slit open. Books, ornaments and my paintings had been thrown on the floor or smashed. The gas and electricity weren't working, and the whole flat was covered in a sticky, smelly mixture of dust and condensation.

I felt embarrassed for Diane to see it like this. She sat down on the sofa, in the cold, dark living room, looking shocked and tearful. After the luxury hotels of the past few days, it seemed like a pit. Worse even than my cell.

Then an old lady who lived a few doors along the balcony showed that not everyone was against me. Mrs Short had heard the noise we made getting through the security door, and came round to welcome us with a little Camping Gaz stove, a plate of sandwiches, hot tea and candles.

Her kindness made everything right. Diane cheered up immediately. The candlelight made things look romantic, so I played my guitar and sang to her. She loved my serenade and got all choked up. We spent that first night lovingly in each other's arms, under some blankets on the floor.

Next morning our first job was to collect my beloved Brandy from the kennels where he'd been transferred after Battersea Dogs Home. It was an emotional moment for me and my faithful friend. He went mad when he saw me, bounding over to jump up and lick my face for the first time in over a year. I was in tears of joy. My little family was now complete.

Yet somehow the press managed to use this happy reunion to snipe at me. They knew I would be picking up my dog as quickly as possible so they staked out the kennels. I didn't mind them taking pictures of us as we brought him out, but some of them wrote that he had failed to recognise me, which was very hurtful.

I wrote letters of complaint, and so did the kennel maids, who confirmed it was complete nonsense. Brandy had been almost begging to be let off the leash to come to me. Our complaints were ignored. I was fair game for any lies. Typical of the rubbish printed about me was some make-believe from a pretty young blonde called Anne-Marie

She lived across the road from me and worked as a stripper. I think I'd said, "Good morning," to her once or twice in my life. Yet she sold a story claiming I'd stalked her on Wimbledon Common while her boyfriend was taking sexy pictures of her. According to this nonsense, she was modelling undies in a secluded part of the common when she spotted me peering through the bushes at her. The fairy tale went on to describe how she screamed, "It's Colin, it's Colin!" and her boyfriend chased me away. It was a complete fabrication. All she wanted was money and publicity off the back of my unwanted infamy.

But I didn't care. My beloved dog was with me again. That was all that mattered. Back home, I got the utilities switched on and we spent the next few days cleaning the flat from top to bottom, making the place habitable. The past was all behind me and I felt I could look forward to settling down with Diane, making a happy home for us both.

Those early days with her were great. They didn't last long, but they were exciting. I was having a lot of sex with a passionate woman, for the first time in my life. Diane was a very experienced lover and introduced me to pleasures I'd never dreamt of. I thought I had an open mind about sex, but she really widened my horizons.

There was also the fun of really getting to know a woman intimately – something I'd never known, or even thought about before. We shared a lot of similar interests in nature, animals, books and New Age beliefs, which made it easier to get close to each other.

While we waited for the newspaper money to come through, we made lists of all the things we needed for our home. It was nice to have someone to look forward to the future with. A big double bed was the first priority, then a car for Diane because I couldn't drive. For the next few weeks we signed on briefly and lived off the bit of money she had saved.

I had hoped to start my new life where it left off, on the day that Rachel died. But there was to be no happy ending for anyone.

Within a week the study window was broken, eggs were thrown at the house and we were sworn at in the street. It became a local game for kids and drunks to run along the balcony at night and kick our door. And we began to get hate mail. Really nasty stuff. It scared us both

There were threats to kill me and Diane – and our children, if we ever had any. I reported them to the police, but they said there was nothing they could do, because there were no clues as to who had sent it. Often it was merely addressed, 'Colin Stagg, Roehampton'. Sometimes there was no stamp and I always refused to pay the postage due. Mostly it was from London, but there were letters from all over the UK.

I tried to make light of it for Diane's sake. "It'll all blow over," I kept telling her. That was wishful thinking. The day my *News of the World* cash came through we went on a shopping spree. On our return, loaded with piles of valuable stuff, we found we'd been burgled. They'd forced the back door and ransacked the place. Luckily, there wasn't much to take. We lost some loose cash and my guitars, and other bits and pieces. It could have been worse. If they'd waited another day they'd have had all our top-of-the-range electrical equipment.

But Diane took it as another sign that the locals were against us. She started to become very loud and aggressive at anything she perceived as a slight or insult – whether it was intended or not. If anyone called us names in the street, she would scream back, "Who do you think you're talking to, you wankers?" or "Come over here and say that, you fucking cowards!"

You've got to understand she was a big, strong girl, with beefy arms covered in tattoos, so she could look quite frightening herself. Nobody ever took up the invitation.

Luckily this sort of confrontation didn't happen too often at first. But it became clear to both of us that there was a lot of anti-Stagg feeling which hadn't gone away after the trial. In fact it had got worse.

I tried to ignore the insults so we could get on with our lives. I bought her a lovely little white Renault 5 so she could get away from Roehampton sometimes. I also took out a life membership in English Heritage for us both, and we used to drive off into the country to visit old ruins, castles and stately homes.

That was brilliant. We shared a love of historic buildings and old ruins, and those days out in the countryside with her and Brandy remain as some of my best memories of our time together.

A couple of times we found a secluded spot and made love on the backseat, then slept in the car. It was wonderful to wake up in the morning, with all the windows steamed up, and drink tea from our flask.

I took her camping once. Sitting wrapped up in blankets around our little fire and gazing up at the stars, which are so much clearer outside the streetlight glow of the cities, it was magical. Brandy had the time of his life, trying to chase rabbits that were far too quick for him. But I think it was a bit too cold and primitive for Diane, because she never wanted to do it again

These were welcome breaks from our life on the Alton estate, where the growing hostility was making life uncomfortable. Apart from the problems outside, we were running short of money. My solicitor had advised me to get rid of the payout as quickly as possible. This was to make myself eligible for Legal Aid, when I started my action against the Metropolitan Police and Paul Britton for malicious prosecution and imprisonment.

Within a month or so of my release, the newspaper money had all gone. I'd handed out about £18,000 to my family, including two of my brothers, nephews, nieces and my mother, who got £6,000. To this day I don't know why I was so generous to her. Nothing she'd done before, during or after my ordeal in jail was for anyone's benefit but her own. But, like a fool, I'd believed her prison visits were signs of belated affection for her son.

Then there was the car and all the luxuries for our home, some clothes for Diane and me, and fairly big donations to the Blue Cross and RSPCA. I also paid off all my debts. Then I signed on again, and immediately ran into the prejudice I've come to accept as normal in my dealings with strangers ever since the trial.

A smarmy young Scot with a thick accent and a superior attitude dealt with my case. He knew exactly who I was and made it clear he thought I was scum. He wanted to know what I had spent the newspaper's money on. I told him it was none of his business. When he asked me what sort of car I owned, I told him I didn't intend to continue the conversation. I was only there to sign on, after all.

Eventually he finished the paperwork and waved his fingers at me, saying, "Go away now." I was furious at his rudeness and called him a few choice names under my breath. This would become typical of the way I was treated.

So there I was. Back where I started. Broke, except for a few hundred I had squirreled away for a rainy day. It didn't matter, because I was going to take the police and their psychologist to the cleaners – or so I thought.

The reality was very different. Over the next four years Legal Aid funded my case against the Met to the tune of nearly £70,000. Like my lawyers, they obviously thought I had a valid case because they invested time and money in me.

But things moved very slowly. Then suddenly, without warning, they turned off the money tap on the grounds that my case had little chance of succeeding. Without this funding I couldn't afford to continue the action. The police were off the hook. I don't believe in conspiracy theories as a rule, but my experience in the Nickell case does make me think that the Establishment stick together.

Being broke again didn't suit Diane. She was a lot more dependent on booze than I'd thought at first. Without a drink she would become surly and sulky. I think she was a borderline alcoholic, and she certainly had a very bad temper. She could also get very jealous, as I soon found out.

Once we had settled in after a couple of weeks, I went to pay my respects to the lady who had written such kind and supportive letters while I was inside. Lee Ashley greeted me like a son and made me welcome. I found her so easy to talk to that

I stayed for hours, and learned she had been in court to hear my acquittal.

Diane wasn't too pleased when I explained she was a kind neighbour who had sent me letters of support in prison. I didn't see Lee again for over a week, until one night when we took the dog out after dark and bumped into her coming home from work.

Diane stayed with Brandy and didn't speak, while I rushed over and hugged her. We chatted for a bit and I invited her to come round and meet my new girlfriend the next evening.

When she arrived, Diane was a bit cool and offhand with her. It wasn't hard to see why. Although Lee was nearly thirty years older, she was tall and slim with a good figure and obviously took pride in herself. Diane, who'd put on a bit of weight, felt the contrast. But her attitude changed when the cash dried up.

Lee was too polite to ever come to see us without calling first. If I answered the phone I would tell her we'd be pleased to see a friendly face. If Diane picked up the call she'd say rudely, "Yeah all right, but make sure you bring a bottle." In later years that changed to, "Make it a big bottle." Lee always put on a pleasant face and never complained. "It's my entrance ticket to the Stagg house," she used to joke.

But other women, some of whom had known me since primary school, weren't so forgiving. If they tried to say 'hello' and chat, Diane would pointedly stand in front of me so they'd have to talk around her. People started saying, "Who does that woman think she is?" It made enemies unnecessarily, and we had enough of those. Apart from a few close neighbours, the attitude around the estate and the surrounding area was overwhelmingly hostile.

I stopped going into most of the local shops because people would stare and whisper who I was to their companions. Sometimes I would place an item on the counter and the assistant would completely ignore me. I would eventually storm out. Even in the big supermarket on the nearby Kingston bypass, I'd be recognised and pointed at. I found this very unnerving.

It forced us to do most of our shopping three miles away, in Worcester Park, but even there my face was known. Diane took it all worse than me. Some of the hate mail had directly threatened to kill her. Coupled with the general anti-Stagg feeling she came to believe her life was at risk. It was to have a devastating effect on our relationship.

Towards Christmas 1994, we were finding it hard to make ends meet. So, after enduring a few days of Diane's sulks, I went upstairs and brought down our reserves. By then I knew how to put her in a good mood. Instantly she was all smiles, and couldn't wait to go out and spend the lot. At least we had some food and drink in the house.

Then the arrival of some sick Christmas greeting cards wiped the smile off her face. Three or four were delivered that called me a murderer and every foul name imaginable, hoping I would soon be dead "like Rachel".

They made Diane even more scared and nervous. At night she kept waking up, thinking someone was trying to get into the flat. I installed extra bolts to calm her fears, and checked all the doors and windows were locked before we went to bed.

Despite these problems it was a good Christmas. The best we had together. My uncle Tony, brother Lee and his wife Carol came for lunch and made a party of it. We had a lovely meal and a lot to drink. It was a proper celebration of my homecoming. 'Fortress Stagg', as I'd come to think of it, was full of real warmth and laughter for the first time in years.

Sadly, it wasn't to last. The tirade of verbal abuse against me continued. Stagg-baiting became a regular sport for the spotty youths who hung around local street corners. They soon realised

Diane would respond angrily to their taunts, and enjoyed winding her up. For all her bluster she became very scared.

Being as it was the party season, there were a lot of drunks rolling home from the pub. They thought it fun to shout out things like, "Come out killer!" and "Slag Stagg!" as they passed. I'd suffered this sort of persecution before, but it was all new to Diane and she wasn't prepared for it. She was convinced someone was going to attack her, so, foolishly, I let her talk me into giving her a weapon for self-defence.

It was an antique naval cosh, from the early 1800s, used by the press gangs on their recruitment drives and given to me by an elderly neighbour years before. Even worse, I agreed to carry a little rusty hand-axe that had been lying out in the garden for years. I didn't *want to*, but she was insistent.

We took to carrying them on our dog walks across the common. Almost inevitably, this led to further trouble. One Sunday morning in mid-January, we were walking round the Queensmere Pond when we passed a man about my age, with a couple of dogs and a young son.

He didn't look at us but muttered, "Wanker!" as he went by. Like an idiot, I lost my cool and turned back towards him. "What the fucking hell's your problem?" I shouted. "Murderer!" he mouthed, and made an obscene gesture at me.

That's when I pulled out the hatchet and shouted, "Do you want some of this then?" I didn't get a chance to say anything else. He threw himself at me, punching and kicking. I dropped the axe and tried to fend him off, but he was too strong

Diane jumped on his back and tried to pull him off me. He didn't care that she was a woman. She was punched hard, headbutted and thrown into the pond for her trouble. I broke away from him to help her out of the water, but he still carried on punching and kicking me.

A park ranger turned up as we were scrapping and meekly told us, "Calm down," then called the police. They couldn't believe their luck. Colin Stagg in an axe attack on Wimbledon Common! They arrived mob-handed, sirens blaring, in five or six squad cars.

Before they turned up, I tossed the axe into the pond. Diane and I were arrested and both charged with carrying an offensive weapon and assault. Of course, we were found guilty and fined. Our assailant had claimed we had made an unprovoked attack on him! He was not charged and quickly sold his story to *The Sun*.

Having been tipped off earlier by the police, their photographer got a picture of a police diver's arm deliberately waving the axe above the surface of the pond. Their headline was 'Axe-calibur'. They described the wimpy ranger as a 'hero'.

The same bloke showed his true colours again three years later. I had just got into Lee Ashley's car after visiting Putney Job Centre when he walked up, opened the passenger door and punched me in the face, saying, "You don't remember me, do you?" I didn't, at first.

As I struggled to get free of the seat belt I became trapped between the door and the kerb, while he rained blows down on me. It was a repeat of the first time we met. When I finally tumbled out he produced a retractable police-style baton and threatened to damage my friend's car, before crossing the road and driving off at the wheel of a London taxi.

We took his number and immediately phoned 999. They advised us to go to the nearest police station to make statements, which we did. I believe he was interviewed, but, despite Lee's eyewitness account of his vicious assault, he was never charged. I wasn't surprised.

Widespread publicity about the axe incident triggered a fresh wave of anti-Stagg feeling. One of the front kitchen windows was smashed, while disgusting phlegm and spittle was daubed across the windscreen and bonnet of our car. Putting the boot into our front door became a weekend sport, along with banging our communal balcony windows.

The garden also made a vulnerable target. It backed on to a wide green space with trees and shrubs between our flats and the tower blocks. Ideal cover for hit-and-run vandals who climbed over the wall and ripped up the flowers. I was worried that they would disturb my dog Sally's grave. A lot of people knew she was buried there – after the police dug her up during their search of the garden – and how much she had meant to me.

But it was the death threats in the post that scared us most. There had been hate mail before, but this was getting really nasty. We came to dread opening the mail. Neither of us wanted to read this poison, but a sort of horrible compulsion made us do it before we burned the letters.

There were some explicit threats to Diane, which included rape and murder. This terrified her so much that I asked Lee if we could stay with her for a few days. It allowed Diane to get a decent night's sleep. At the top of a tower block, with access by entry-phone, she didn't feel so vulnerable and I didn't have to get up to check that every strange noise wasn't a break-in.

This kindness helped her and Lee to become friends. We invited her over a lot during the following months, and always had a good time. Those evenings helped us forget the hostility waiting outside our front door.

Both of us had signed on again on and even that simple procedure brought its dangers. We often suffered verbal abuse at the Job Centre, and both of us came to hate going there. But we needed the money, even if a lot of it went on Diane's booze. I started drinking more too, just to keep her company, but after I reached a certain point I didn't enjoy it that much. Lee used to bring us little treats – a bottle of wine, or a takeaway and food for Brandy. She also helped us out with cash from time to time.

To be fair, Diane did keep a record of these sums, but once she sussed that Lee had savings she started wanting to borrow money. One night she asked for a loan of £1,000. I could see Lee was embarrassed, and so was I. Lee said she only had £400 available, so Diane sniffed, "That's no good to me," and went off to bed in a huff like a spoilt child.

I think Lee was very relieved. But Diane mulled this over during the night. The first thing next morning, she made me phone up and say she had changed her mind and we would take the £400 loan after all!

I sill owe Lee that money, and a lot more. Once Diane left, she helped me out time and time again. Without her kindness and unselfish support I don't know how I would have survived on the pittance of dole money all these years

Back then, the money was a lifeline. It helped to keep Diane happily in booze for a while, but the strain of living in constant fear was getting to her. She was taking Valium for depression, then mixing it with alcohol. The result was mood swings and temper tantrums, which became worse with each new threat to us.

I should have recognised that the writing was on the wall for our relationship that spring. Although I still cared for her a lot, the strain of living with the private rows and the public hate campaign was getting too much. But instead of cutting my losses, and admitting this wasn't going to work, I ignored my gut instinct and allowed myself to be bullied into a disastrous marriage.

There was a simple reason for this. I didn't want to be left on my own. Not then, when all the world seemed to have turned against me. However frightening things became, it would be easier to bear if there were two of us.

ELEVEN

Diane started talking more seriously about marriage, as the true scale of public feeling against me was revealed in the New Year. By then we were both in fear for our lives. I learned what the rabbit feels like – cowering in its burrow with the fox outside, waiting to pounce. That was us.

Every time we went out there was the risk of running into trouble. Diane's biggest fear was that something terrible would happen to me, and she would be left homeless. I tried to reassure her that it would never come to that, but she wouldn't be comforted. In the end I had her name put on the rent book. It's still there. I never bothered to change it after she left.

But even this didn't satisfy her. She kept saying we loved each other and should get married. It was the only way she could be sure her tenancy would be protected, and being a widow would make it easier for her in all sorts of ways. I told her she sounded certain I was going to die.

By this stage I still wasn't too sure how I felt. I thought I loved her, but I was really *in lust* with her. I liked her a lot and had great affection for her. It was just that marriage seemed a step too far for me.

We had only been together physically for about six months, and our situation wasn't exactly ideal. I was probably the most hated man in the country, she had a massive drink problem and we hadn't a penny between us.

I hadn't expected the question to arise because, from her letters to me in jail, I knew she was still married to someone called Beddoes. They had been separated for years and she'd reverted to her maiden name. She said they lost touch long ago and she had no way of reaching him. That seemed to rule out remarriage until she got a divorce. I hoped it would take forever.

Diane had different ideas. Unknown to me, she made moves to track down her husband. She surprised herself – and me – when she found him quickly, and he was as eager to make their long separation permanent as she was. It removed her main obstacle to getting married, and she redoubled her efforts to persuade me. It was like being steamrollered and brainwashed at the same time. She never let up.

I used to confide my doubts to Lee, who gave me some very practical advice. I had to ask myself the key question, 'Do I truly want to marry her?' If I didn't, then I should be prepared to lose her – because Diane wasn't going to settle for anything less.

Whatever decision I made, I had to make it with my eyes wide open. Her drinking, that was always going to be a problem. She was an alcoholic, and her first loyalty was to the bottle. When I told Lee that Di had promised to cut down once we were married, she laughed at it – unlike me, she knew that alkies never change.

About a week after this, I invited Lee to come over one evening. As she walked through the hall Di was coming down the stairs, pissed and in a foul temper. Taking one look at our visitor, she grunted, "You here again, why don't you fuck off?"

Lee smiled sweetly and replied, "You know, darling, I think I will," and walked out. As I tried to apologise for her rudeness, she warned me, "Remember Colin, this is what you have to look forward to."

I mulled these words over for a long time, weighing up what I wanted against what the future would really hold. All the while Diane kept up her relentless pressure, while the eggs and bootmarks kept staining and scratching our front door.

Finally I gave in and agreed to her proposal. The thought of losing her was too much. After being a loner all my life and spending virtually a year in solitary on remand, I finally had someone to share with.

I knew this woman was fiercely loyal and protective of me. We had many interests in common, and I thought I could curb her boozing. So I in the end I said 'yes', to keep the peace and her company.

For a while she became the bubbly, fun-loving woman I had first met. Even her night terrors disappeared. Wedding plans filled her life and left no room for fear. The divorce was in the pipeline, and she arranged a wedding date for August 15th at Wandsworth Town Hall. I couldn't get caught up in Diane's excitement, as I still had lingering doubts. But her first hurdle before the altar was cleared on May 26th, when Lee accompanied her to court for the quickie divorce hearing.

Three nights later, we were reminded of the dangerous reality of our situation. It began with our front door being kicked repeatedly, and loud swearing. Diane begged me not to go outside. She was terrified. While I was calming her down with a large drink, they smashed the kitchen window.

We called the police, who eventually turned up, gave us a crime number, said there were no witnesses and there was nothing they could do. (One of them suggested the best thing for us was to move away!)

After sitting up half the night with little sleep, I phoned Lee in the morning and begged her to let us stay with her again for a couple of days. Lee invited us round immediately, and Diane went straight to bed at eleven in the morning. She was shattered. I grabbed a few hours sleep myself later on, after Lee had cooked us a meal.

But by midnight I was on my way back home, after Diane and I had a terrible row. "She's started on me again. I can't take any more," I told Lee as I stormed out. It was lucky for the Stagg-baiters that they didn't meet me that night as I walked Brandy home, given the black mood I was in.

I can't even recall what the row was about – probably her drinking, or not having any money because she was drinking so much. Lee had been woken by our shouting. She tried to reason with her and was told by Di, "Bollocks to you – I'm going to smash the car up!" Then she stormed off after me.

That must have taken some courage, because she would never willingly go out at night by herself. We made up eventually and went back to Lee's. After apologising to her next morning, we stayed for another two nights.

There was some good news for me around this time, as the Legal Aid application to fund a civil action against the police had finally been approved. The pleasure was short-lived, however, when the *Mail on Sunday*, which still treated me as prime suspect in the Nickell case, carried a story full of objections to it. That whipped up more public hatred towards me. The threats and verbal abuse always escalated after one of these stories appeared. And they kept on coming.

I was always described in derogatory terms as a 'sick weirdo', a 'pervert', a 'kinky sex offender' who dabbled in the occult and lived in a 'squalid council flat' with 'black painted walls', hung with knives and satanic symbols. For a decade there was what I can only describe as a sustained and vicious press campaign against me.

Even today, these snide little tags are sometimes used in headlines or the introduction to stories about me. It's as if I was typecast as a villain all those years ago and nobody really wants to change the casting.

Then, in that summer of '95, we had a slice of luck. We were approached by Sky TV to do a *UK Living* interview. It paid £175, so we jumped at the chance to tell people how miserable our lives had been made.

But it didn't have any effect. A few weeks later was the third anniversary of Rachel's murder, and I was dreading the inevitable newspaper articles about it. Sure enough, the *Mail on Sunday* ridiculed our TV appearance under the headline 'Rise of a Nobody', and other titles carried stories about the case and my involvement. Our wedding plans were in full swing right then, but the death-threat letters that followed the articles took the gloss right off them.

There seemed no end to it. Di started suffering a lot of stomach pain, and thought she either had a cyst or an ulcer brought by the terrible hate mail and the threats of violence. And I was feeling trapped. I almost called the wedding off when we went to meet the registrar to go over some details, four days before the ceremony.

I suddenly blurted out, "I don't want to get married." That caused a stir. The poor man suggested we go outside and talk about it, before things went any further. Di was furious. I sounded like a kid when I told her, "I don't want to be married. I want to go home, I have a jigsaw to finish." It sounds laughable now, but

I really didn't want to do it. But like a kid, I was given no choice. As I was dragged back into the town hall, I kept muttering about how years ago, among the poorer classes, all you had to do to get married was jump on a bottle.

The wedding had already caused problems with my best man. My brother Lee had the job until a couple of weeks before the wedding. But my sister-in-law, Carol, made him step down. She was so frightened he might appear in the papers and make them into hate targets too that she refused to come. It meant my brother couldn't attend either.

I wouldn't wish my situation on anybody, so I asked an old school friend, Martin Butler, to do the honours. But he only lasted a few days in the role before his wife and mother ganged up to make him drop out, too. To make things worse, Martin looked a bit like me and had been briefly pulled in for questioning at the time of the murder. But at least he turned up for the wedding.

Eventually I got his brother, David, who had been off work with a back injury. He was a Jack–the–Lad sort of bloke and laughed off any dangers.

Our big day approached and I was dreading it. The night before, Diane started celebrating early and got pissed out of her head. We had a massive row over her drinking and she passed out on the bed. While she slept, I went downstairs and poured a litre bottle of Scotch down the sink. It was a wedding present from Big Tony in the flat above ours, who was one of my few sympathisers. I didn't like to waste his gift, but I was so angry.

I spent the night on the couch, with hardly a wink of sleep, and was up early. I sat on the steps leading down to the garden as dawn broke, smoking and thinking how mad I must have been to be doing this. When she finally staggered downstairs, bleary-eyed and hung-over, another row started over me emptying the whisky bottle.

In the middle of all this, the registrar called to warn us there were a lot of press outside the town hall. He advised us it would be better to postpone the ceremony until Monday, when he would fit us in quietly. That sobered Di up fast. She insisted on going ahead *now* – never mind the media. She told me later that she thought if I didn't say, "I do" on that very day then I never would.

She was probably right. So against my better judgement I surrendered to the inevitable. I've only myself to blame. For almost a year I'd known what I was getting into. I had been warned what was likely to happen, and yet I still walked into marriage with my eyes wide shut.

There was one more little drama before we left. Diane tried to make Lee stay behind at the flat to look after Brandy. This was the woman who had helped her make all the preparations, paid for lots of bits and pieces and lent us money. I put my foot down, and so did the neighbour who was taking us there in his limo. He refused to go without Lee, so she sat upfront in the wedding car.

Dozens of press and TV were waiting for us. But, thanks to a jobsworth parking attendant, we had to go home again. We had forgotten the special pass that allowed us to use the council car park inside the town hall, and he refused us entry without it. Di thought I had done it deliberately.

In the end I made it up the aisle with the minimum of fuss. I had resigned myself to getting married and decided to try to make the best of it. After a good old-fashioned knees-up reception party, we settled down to our life as the Staggs at number sixteen.

Our marriage limped along in fits and starts for another two years, and coincided with some of the blackest moments of my life. Di's behaviour played its part in these dismal times. But it was the unrelenting press and public hatred over the following seven or eight years which sapped my spirits.

At least with Diane I knew what to expect and, until the break-up, I could count on her unswerving loyalty. With the outside world it was a constant fear of the unexpected. And the drip, drip, drip of abuse was like Chinese water torture, wearing me down until I came close to cracking.

Unless you experience it for yourself, it's impossible to convey the full devastating effect. The closest comparison I can think of is with our troops on patrol in Iraq and Afghanistan. Never able to relax, living under constant threat of attack. That was us.

Of course Di broke her promise to curb the drinking. Her excuse was that being Mrs Stagg made her live in fear of being attacked, and the drink dulled that fear. I thought this was a bit rich, considering how hard she'd pressed me to get married.

I think she found it hard to live with a man who didn't get drunk with her. She was a party animal who liked noise and people around her all the time. Loud rows followed by passionate making-up seemed normal to her. I was all for the quiet life, sitting at home, watching TV, playing the guitar or listening to music.

The novelty of sex was starting to wear off as well. What had started off as an open-all-hours sweetshop was now becoming a bit of a chore. I kept myself reasonably fit, working out in my home gym, but her demands were exhausting. She wanted to go on for hours at a time, in every position on the compass.

Di's drinking didn't help. It's off-putting to make love to a drunk who complains half the time that you're not giving her all she wants. So one night, early in our marriage, I decided to do exactly what she wanted. I gave her the full Monty for hours on end.

Next morning I brought her breakfast in bed, and confidently asked, "Did you enjoy yourself last night?" She looked up at me with bloodshot eyes and replied, "I dunno. I can't remember a thing about it. I was too pissed." That was a real turn-off.

Throughout that autumn, it became clear that she had neither the intention nor the will to give up drinking. After a couple of months she was back to her old habits.

Meanwhile, it was difficult enough trying to make ends meet. Finding work was impossible. Prospective employers would take one look at my name and the vacancy would be mysteriously filled. Diane, on the other hand, made no attempt to get a job. She told me she had worked solidly for seven years, and now she was going to put her feet up. Her excuse to the Job Centre was the one she used to justify getting drunk - as my wife, she would always be at risk.

But this meant we only had our dole money and the small amounts we could borrow, or earn on the side. That alone couldn't pay for her drink, or leave anything over for the home. It became a struggle to survive.

Towards the end of the year, Di announced that we were "cancelling Christmas". The arrival of five or six hate-filled cards had unsettled her badly. One read, "To the murderer. How can you sleep at night? And how can that fat whore sleep with you? Does she like it with a pervert? Do you call her Rachel?" Di was desperate to get away after that. She was convinced they were coming to get us, and so, without the money to go anywhere else, we went to my brother Lee's.

It was a very bad time for me. I got deeply depressed at the way people treated us. There was no money, no job, and my home life was a series of drunken rows. I remember thinking, "If this is the best that life can offer, it stinks!"

And in early 1996 it got even worse. My faithful dog Brandy – the only creature that wanted nothing from me except love and affection, and repaid me in kind – died. I was distraught, blinded by tears as I buried him in the back garden. The last link with what had been a mundane yet happy existence was gone.

Diane understood my misery, and tried to persuade me to get a new pet as quickly as possible to fill the void. I couldn't bear the thought of another dog at first, but after a couple of months she persuaded me. She and Lee went off to Battersea Dogs Home – but without me. I knew that seeing these poor abandoned creatures would be too upsetting. I would want to bring them all home.

So two hours later they phoned me to ask for my choice between a black Labrador and a black and white collie. "I'll take the black Lab," I told them. That was how Gipsy joined our family. A few months later, a neighbour presented me with another black Labrador puppy I called Jessie. These two lovely animals would provide some of my only warmth and comfort in the years ahead.

Diane loved them. And soon after bringing Gipsy home she had something else to smile about. She found her dream job – as a sex-line chat hostess! One of our neighbours happened to mention that some women on the estate talked dirty down the phone to earn a bit of extra money. That was all Di needed to hear.

Within days she had tracked down these women, got in touch with the locally based firm and, after an audition, was taken on. It was ideal for her because it meant she could work from her own sitting room, for whichever hours she chose. The more hours on call the more money she could earn. It depended on how many people were put through from the main switchboard.

They gave her a special phone code for when she was working. This clocked up the premium line minutes the callers spent. Di's job was to keep them on as long as possible. And she was brilliant. She called herself Jade, and very soon the punters were asking to be connected to her by name.

Putting on a huskily seductive tone – nothing like her normal speaking voice – she played their libidos like a virtuoso violinist. She pretended to be a bored housewife, whose husband was away working on the oil rigs, and she was gagging for sex. But she would switch roles, depending what she thought they wanted.

Starting around midday, she would often work an afternoon shift and then late evening and early morning. I would cook her meals and bring in her favourite Bacardi and Coke, while she sat there waiting for the phone to ring.

It could be quite a turn-on, listening to only her half of the conversations. In the early days, when she worked longer, she was also picking up over well £100 a week cash-in-hand. It could also be a bit of a laugh. She'd be telling some bloke how she was lying in bed on black silk sheets, slowly pulling her negligee up over her thighs. In reality she was wrapped up like a bag lady, in bed socks, tracksuit bottoms, woolly jumper and dressing gown, more often than not signalling for a fresh drink.

But the novelty gradually wore off. I started to feel a bit like a pimp, and the things she was saying to these strangers made me uncomfortable. One of her regulars, who claimed to be an Italian millionaire, wanted to meet her in the flesh. I actually think she was tempted, because in our rows she would threaten to run off with this wealthy bloke. I pointed out that a millionaire wouldn't be bothered with bored housewives on a second rate sex-line. That didn't go down well.

Still, the money was useful. It enabled us to buy a few things for the flat, a lot more drink and, above all, it kept her from brooding about our situation. The sulks and surly behaviour didn't happen so often. It also allowed her to invite the neighbours in for parties. But inevitably she would get pissed and end up upsetting someone.

She kept doing it for over a year, but towards the end the pay wasn't so good when she didn't put the hours in. Like a lot of things she started, Diane got bored with it. But it ended because of a party she threw for other chat-line women. They had got to know each other and used to swap stories about the punters who called them. Diane had the idea for a get-together and a lot of them were enthusiastic. As well as the locals, some came from as far away as Portsmouth and Essex.

I had the time of my life. It wasn't Diane they had come to see – it was me! When they discovered Diane was married to the infamous Colin Stagg, they couldn't wait to meet me! Although some of them brought their husbands and boyfriends, others came by themselves and made it very plain they were available. Everybody brought booze, so the place was awash with it.

And the women were flirting outrageously with me. One of them, who had come with her husband, even wanted Diane and me to make a foursome and swap partners. With the mood I was in I wouldn't have minded, but Diane turned them down. She was feeling jealous at the attention I was already getting.

The party went on into the small hours, and some of them stayed over. I thought it was great. For once, I'd been able to forget all my troubles and just revel in being the centre of attention in a way that didn't involve being threatened or sworn at. But there was a price to pay.

One of them tipped off the *News of the World* about Diane's sex-line work and me chatting up the chat girls. A story appeared a week later. Diane lost her job and it touched off another outbreak of anti-Stagg feeling. It left her despondent. We were only gradually recovering from the last burst of hostility.

The job had been good for her in a lot of ways. It had given her something to do with her time, and the money she brought in was a useful bonus in that summer of 1996. She became a lot happier, which indirectly led to her new obsession – having a baby, "to make us a proper family," as she put it. I thought she was mad.

Apart from the obvious financial cost, there was the public backlash that was sure to follow. Bringing up a child while we lived under constant threat would be impossible. I didn't want to put any child of mine at risk.

Like everything else, she just batted my objections aside. She was going to have a baby and nothing was going to stop her. And to ensure it happened, I was forced to increase my marital duties.

But nothing happened. Tests revealed her tubes were damaged and she was unlikely to conceive normally. The only option left to us was IVF treatment, which would cost about £1,400.

Di was still determined to go ahead, and insisted she would work longer hours to save up the money. But before treatment could begin she had to take a number of tests. The result was that she had to lose weight and stop smoking and drinking. They gave her a couple of months to lose a stone. Initially, she did shed a few pounds. But drink took preference over a child, and eventually she dropped the whole idea in favour of her old habits.

That meant almost no exercise other than lifting a glass. Spending days and nights on the sofa, talking dirty, stuffing herself with food and drink, her weight ballooned.

Things were generally quieter for us at this time. There were the usual stories on the anniversary of the murder and the usual hate letters, but nothing really nasty. Things settled down a bit, until the *Daily Mail* announced in September that the Nickells were planning a civil action against me – a 'scoop' instantly demolished when Andrew Nickell denied any such plan. But 'Black October' brought out the nutters and Stagg-haters in their droves.

It started on the 15th when Andre Hanscombe made an appearance on the *Richard and Judy* show, talking about the murder and its aftermath for him and little Alex. He warned that the killer might strike again, then ended by saying, "The sight of Colin Stagg being released from the Old Bailey was almost worse for me than Rachel's murder."

The intensity of this man's hatred of me was, and still is, frightening. He has clung to the belief that I killed the love of his life. I've tried to make allowances for the grief he and his son have suffered, but it's hard.

I have wondered if he's hiding a sense of guilt at allowing her to take walks on local common ground, where she'd been accosted several times before her death. But that sounds like something Paul Britton might say, and I'm no psychologist.

His broadcast inflamed all the old animosities towards me. There were death-threat letters and people called me out in the street. Within a few days it got even worse. My old enemies at the *Mail on Sunday* carried a three-page spread under the headline, "The case against Colin Stagg' a jury never heard." It was a thinly disguised accusation of murder, and it was grossly distorted. Witness statements from people like Lillian Avid, Susan Gale, Amanda Phelan and Jane Harriman were paraded with a theatrical flourish and presented as damning, solid evidence of my guilt.

What the paper omitted to mention was that the CPS had regarded their evidence as far too weak to justify charging me, after my first arrest in September 1992. They dare not use my letters to Lizzie because they would have had to publish *her letters to me*. That would have clearly shown how I was manipulated by the police and their psychologist.

Instead they cited selected parts of her testimony and twisted a vital fact to suit their scenario. On our last meeting in Hyde Park, I had demonstrated how I thought Rachel's hands were clasped together, prayer-like, in the photo I'd been shown by detectives.

The prosecution had claimed this was vital evidence that amounted to a confession, because her hands were not visible in the photo. Only the killer could have known their true position. But the judge had sharply pointed out that I'd got it wrong. Her hands were crossed *at the wrist*. In his view, this removed an important plank of the prosecution case.

The paper ignored his remarks and wrote, "He described how her hands were crossed as if in prayer." This was one big distortion, but there was nobody to challenge it. There's no defence in trial by media. The *Mail on Sunday* carefully chose what it needed to justify its story before acting as judge and jury.

Nobody cared about that. It was open season on the Staggs. This was the first time any evidence about the case had ever been reported, and every other paper picked up on the story. The committal had restricted press coverage to a bare outline of the charge, and the trial ended before it began – so now there was intense public interest.

It also touched off a sustained hate campaign and another media scrum. On the Sunday morning this article appeared we were soon under siege. The first reporter knocked on the door about 8am. He gave Di a copy of the paper and asked for our comments. She brought it in to me and freaked out.

One look at the headline told me why she was so upset. As I read through the piece I got more and more angry. It was a combination of the circumstantial evidence the CPS had declined to take to trial on my first arrest and the Lizzie James evidence the judge had savaged and dismissed.

There was no cross-examination, no defence, no rebuttal, no expert witnesses for my side. It was a pure hatchet job. I stormed out onto the balcony and set fire to the paper, shouting, "This is a pack of lies! They're fitting me up again!" Then I ran back inside and slammed the door.

I was shaking with rage and fear. I knew this would bring out all the crazies against me. They had painted a great big target on me. And there was nothing I could do to remove it.

By 9am at least sixty or seventy press people were milling about outside. There was a big group of photographers and TV cameras set up across the street from the front door, waiting for me to come out. It was insane. Reporters were running around the estate like demented rats, trying to interview anybody mentioned in the witness statements.

They kept banging on my door, and even climbed up on the garden wall at the rear of the flat trying to take pictures through the back windows. Some of my near neighbours who were on my side came out onto the balconies to remonstrate with them. There was shouting and swearing and near punch-ups. It was worse than the pack outside the Old Bailey, because this was my home and this time I'd been portrayed as guilty as charged.

Michelle from next door and Big Tony from the flat upstairs came down to give us support and to chase off the most intrusive reporters. At one point Tony went outside, carrying the diary I had written in prison along with my comments on the case. He was waving this above his head and shouting, "If you want to know the true story you'll have to buy his book! It's all in here," but there were no takers.

By lunchtime Di had started drinking and was getting more aggressive by the minute. She wanted to go outside and take on the press. I tried to stop her. It was just what the bastards wanted. But there was no stopping her in that mood. She had the idea of spraying them with our garden hose. It was a good idea but unfortunately the hose was leaking, and when she staggered outside onto the walkway, effing and blinding, only a dribble came out. That gave them a picture but they still weren't satisfied.

We had to wait them out. So we stayed indoors, hoping they would finally get fed up and move off. In the meantime I needed a drink myself. It seemed liked the newspapers wouldn't be satisfied until I was dead.

There was only one bright spot in that day. I got a bit tipsy and took a petty revenge for being held prisoner in my own home.

By tea-time most of them had given up, but there were a few left, parked up in cars down the road. I sneaked out the back and walked round the block to come up behind one of them.

I had made a poster reading, "I'm a prick" and Sellotaped it to the boot of their car without them noticing. It was silly, but satisfying. But they had the last laugh. Next morning similar versions of the 'unheard case' story were in every paper, and the reporters and photographers were back outside my door.

The story rumbled on for days and the hate mail soon started arriving: nine letters, including death threats. A request to appear on the Richard Littlejohn TV show came too, and we foolishly agreed. I thought I could put my side of the story, and the £400 fee would come in very handy. It was a forlorn hope. They knew how to get their money's worth.

The show was designed as a gladiatorial arena. Within minutes of arriving we realised our role was to be thrown to the 'pitbulls'. The audience seemed to be made up of bikers, punks and followers of sadomasochism. They were a rough, foul-mouthed bunch and we refused to sit with them for fear of violence.

That didn't save us. The questioning was confrontational and I took the bait, jumping up and ranting at my tormentors. Good telly, bad image for the Staggs. In a bid to set the record straight we accepted another proposal, soon afterwards, to cooperate in making a programme for the respected *Cook Report*.

They wanted me to take another lie detector test on camera and examine the strengths and weaknesses of the case against me. In truth I didn't think it would make much difference. The general public had made up its collective mind about me. Only finding the real killer would change that – and maybe not even then . . .

The true appeal of the Cook show was it would take us away from Roehampton. They wanted to stash us in a country cottage up in the Midlands, to be nearer their Birmingham studios. It would get us away until the storm whipped up by the *Mail* story, hopefully calmed down, and they gave us £2,000 for our expenses.

We stayed in a remote valley near Ludlow. The cottage had beams and an open fireplace with beautiful walking places all around for the dogs. After the ordeal of the previous weeks it was like paradise. As near to a proper holiday as I had ever had. Lee and the dogs came too, along with a minder who turned out to be a great cook. (He and Di were always fighting for the stove. Luckily for us he always won.)

The only hiccups were when I was recognised, firstly on a trip to Ludlow Castle and later as we walked back to the studios in the centre of Birmingham. There was no threat of violence or any sign of hostility, but it was unnerving and confirmed my fears that I could be recognised wherever I went.

I passed the lie detector test, but I refused to take a truth drug because I have a strong aversion to both drugs and needles. I did agree to be hypnotised, but the hypnotist couldn't put me under the 'fluence.

The broadcast, shortly before Christmas, was fairly even-handed but didn't go very far towards clearing my name. Di was disappointed, but I didn't care too much. I was becoming immune to anything written or broadcast about me. Their fee meant we had enough food and drink for the holiday season, and for a while we didn't have to worry about money.

One very interesting admission did emerge from Keith Pedder. He was challenged by one of the show's sharpest journalists, who had spent days reading the full witness statements from everyone quoted in the *Mail on Sunday* story. "You can't seriously suggest there's anything in that lot which would have got a conviction. There's nothing linking him to the murder. It's only circumstantial at best. Good defence would have ripped them to shreds," he told Pedder.

To his amazement, the ex- DI replied: "You're quite right. It wouldn't have got to court. But the Lizzie James letters made all the difference. The paper didn't run them." And that's what the *Mail*'s case really boiled down to: A lot of half-baked circumstantial evidence that wouldn't have survived cross-examination, plus a distorted piece of my testimony.

This year, there were the usual seasonal hate cards as the backlash from the story continued. But there was a lot worse to come.

TWELVE

One by-product of *The Cook Report* was that a sleazy filmmaker and a slippery crime writer crawled out of the woodwork. They tried to cash in on my notoriety and inadvertently put the skids under my marriage, when their money-making scheme folded.

Soon after the TV broadcast, I was approached by Barrie Goulding, the man behind the sick video hits *Live Operations* and *Executions*. He had made a fortune from these downmarket compilation tapes of patients' innards, beheadings, shootings and hangings. And he smelled some more in putting me on film.

Together with his partner Christopher Berry-Dee, a self-professed criminologist and true crime author, he proposed a violent video reconstruction of Rachel's murder, to be filmed on Wimbledon Common. They also planned a TV version of 'The Trial That Never Was' using my witness statements, a retired judge and barristers, with the verdict by viewers' phone-ins – from which they would take a percentage!

It all sounded a bit farfetched, but they said they had already received a lot of interest in the £250,000 project from Anglia TV's head of features and current affairs. More importantly, Goulding promised us £1,000 if we agreed to their plans in principle and attended an exploratory meeting with the Anglia people.

Berry-Dee also showed a lot of interest in the book I'd started writing while in prison. He said he could help me by ghost-writing it into a best-seller. Like a fool I let him persuade me to hand over a lot of documents, including the original Lizzie James letters, post-mortem reports and police files plus my own manuscript. I should have followed my instincts.

He was one of those middle-aged blokes who think it's trendy to have long hair, wear loads of bling and drive a clapped-out XJ6. He even claimed to be a descendent of Dr John Dee, the mysterious necromancer and spy for Queen Elizabeth I. (Personally I thought he was a smarmy bullshitter.)

But he seemed to offer a way to get my book published, which would give my side of the story and hopefully make people see me in a better light. The penny dropped when our promised fee repeatedly failed to materialise, and Anglia ditched the project when no other TV network showed interest in buying it.

Then we were tipped off that this pair were going around Fleet Street behind our backs, touting my documents to the highest bidder for an asking price of £30,000 to £35,000! Goulding was saying to news executives: "The Lizzie letters are amazing. Pornographic. You should read the things she says she wanted Stagg to do to her." Berry-Dee told one news editor: "He trusts me completely and has become dependent on me. With Colin I just have to press the right buttons.

"I've got right inside his head. I have even offered to take him to Thailand where he could have a great time fucking his brains out.

"Being with Stagg is akin to standing on a rumbling volcano that is ready to explode. I think he is ready to blow at any moment."

And this from only two meetings with the man. Di went mental when she heard about what he had said. She was always madly jealous, and thought I'd been planning a Far Eastern 'lads only' holiday without her. I wasn't too pleased either, when I was told what Goulding had been saying about me. "It's strange. I found myself warming to him. I couldn't help it," he told another executive. "But afterwards, when I thought about it, shaking his hand and all that, and what he was accused of doing, I felt dreadful. I had to get my wife to stop the car for me to be sick." This from a man who made money out of a beheading!

I didn't want anything more to do with this pair of chancers. I needed to get my documents back and forget the whole thing. That proved easier said than done. But Diane wouldn't let it rest. She was still furious with me over the 'Thai trip' nonsense and she'd had a sniff of big money to be made.

We had a series of rows which went on and on, about *us* selling the letters ourselves. I didn't mind using them in a book, but if a newspaper published them there would have been a public backlash. And I already knew to my cost how bad that could be.

But when Diane walked out it shocked the life out of me. I couldn't believe she had left me. She only took a few things with her, and said she would be back for the rest later. When I tried to stop her going she threatened to call the police.

I was totally gutted. She had nowhere to go and not much money. For some reason, I kept getting these images of her being attacked and lying injured in a back alley. I was close to losing my reason for worry.

I had good reason to, but not for the reasons I thought. Unbeknownst to me, she was knocking back the brandy and enjoying five-star treatment at a posh Kensington hotel, courtesy of the *Mail on Sunday*. The crafty cow had secretly got in touch with them and done a deal to sell her 'Secrets of Life with Colin Stagg'. It must have cost them a fortune just wining and dining her for three days and nights while two reporters interviewed her.

Back in Roehampton I was close to a breakdown. After more than two years I was accustomed to sharing my home. Suddenly it seemed empty again, and even the dogs couldn't take her place. I hated the rows and the drinking. The surly sulks and fits of temper. But there were still tender moments and fun. To tell the truth, I missed her badly, which was why I kept getting nightmare images of her being hurt

My friend Lee came round to console me and offer words of comfort. She told me Diane could look after herself and it would be a brave mugger or rapist who tried to take her on.

By the weekend I had calmed down a lot, and self-pity had been replaced by rage at her dumping me for no apparent reason. I threw a bit of a tantrum, taking all her clothes outside and burning them in the garden. It was a symbolic gesture. I was erasing her from my life.

So when she turned up in a taxi on Sunday morning, with a couple of bottles, a copy of the paper and a big smile, it was a shock. It had all been part of a big surprise by her, fooling the papers and earning us some money – or so she said. I was so pleased to see her I welcomed her with open arms. She wasn't so happy when she found out I'd destroyed her whole wardrobe, but said we had enough now to buy her a new one.

I wasn't too pleased to read that she'd run away to avoid my 'violent outbursts'. I thought that was rich coming from a belligerent drunk. But I kept my mouth shut. She'd also made up a lot of rubbish about how I sometimes scared her, and how she'd begun to think I might have murdered Rachel after all.

This worried me, because it was the sort of thing that would cause a fresh outbreak of Stagg-bashing. Then the press pack started to arrive, looking for follow-up stories, which justified my fears.

There were some vicious letters too, but very little trouble on the estate. Most people there knew what a loudmouthed drunk Di could be. If anyone was going to be bashed up in our flat, they thought it would be me

We picked up the threads of our lives, but it was never the same again. Life without Di, even for a short while, had been miserable, but life with her wasn't that good any more. She no longer worked the sex-chat line, since she'd been exposed in the papers after we hosted the party for the chat-line women.

I think it also had a lot to do with being pandered to by the *Cook Report* people and then the *Mail on Sunday*, who had wanted to keep her sweet. They had also given her a glimpse of a life beyond the Alton Estate, where she could relax and enjoy herself without the constant stress of being Mrs Stagg.

For the first time she was mixing with men and women who had a lot going for them. They knew how to enjoy themselves, they were interesting and they didn't live with a sense of fear, banged up on a rundown council estate.

Apart from settling back in with Di, my main concern was getting my papers back from Berry-Dee, who wasn't best pleased by her story. (It had denied him a big payday.) He stopped answering my phone calls and ignored my letters. In the end I put my solicitor onto him, and managed to get my book back. But he kept the Lizzie letters, and I couldn't afford to chase him any further.

I had more problems on the home front. Di's behaviour was spiralling out of control. Her drunken antics had even antagonised the neighbours who'd stuck up for me. Police were being called regularly to deal with our rows and her belligerent behaviour out in the street. It caused more antagonism towards me, and sparked off a fresh round of threats and attacks on our home.

My staunchest supporter, Big Tony from upstairs, became so fearful for his family's safety that he asked the council for a move. Within two weeks he was gone. That's how seriously the council took the risk.

Our next-door neighbour Michelle, her closest friend, wouldn't have anything to do with us. She had invited us to a barbecue but made the mistake of telling Di off for pouring lighter fuel on the coals and almost setting fire to her kids. Di festered over this imagined slight for a few days, then wrote an anonymous letter claiming Michelle was dealing drugs and holding loud all-night parties.

This was pushed through about twenty neighbourhood doors. It was all lies, but someone passed it on to the council and Michelle almost lost her home. I knew nothing about it but Michelle blamed both of us. Within weeks we were isolated. Only Lee stood up for me. Di was rude and ungrateful to her too (unless she wanted a loan), and I had to keep apologising for her behaviour to keep my only real friend.

Home life was becoming a nightmare. The rows and her drinking left me emotionally drained. Then she disappeared again and I was plunged into despair. Despite everything that had been going wrong I never thought she would really leave.

In my panic I kept imagining the worst again. It was tearing me apart. Again, I pictured her lying raped, or even dead, attacked because she was recognised as 'Mrs Stagg', or had been sounding off in some pub. There was no consoling me. I was going frantic. This was much worse than her first disappearance.

But I could have spared myself the heartache. A few nights later she turned up at Lee's flat, and proceeded to drink almost a bottle of Scotch to give her the courage to ask me to take her back.

I met her outside our back gate and just flung my arms around her. I was so relieved that she was safe. But my happiness lasted less than a minute. A bloke walked past us on the path and she freaked. "He's a photographer!" she screamed. "Get him, get him!"

I tried to explain it was only an innocent passer-by, but I couldn't pacify her and she turned on me "You're not a man. A real man would defend his woman!" she shouted. I didn't realise how much booze she'd consumed; so to keep the peace, I agreed to go and confront the bloke while she made her way round the front and went indoors.

But instead she started shouting and swearing outside Michelle's front window, until the police turned up. While all this was going on, I was taking a leisurely stroll. I had no intention of tackling anyone. I was just giving her time to calm down.

When I came in through the back of the flat I could hear her outside, shouting the odds at the police. About a dozen of them had arrived in several patrol cars and a big van. They were going to need them. By now she was out of control.

Their attempts to quieten her down failed. Finally they lost patience and decided to arrest her. She had pulled one drunken stunt too many. What happened next was a treat for the big audience who'd come out onto the balconies for a ringside view.

Di was a big strong girl who weighed about fifteen stone by then, and she wasn't going quietly. Those beefy arms packed a punch and it took seven of them to finally subdue her. In the melee she kicked one of them very hard, which brought the serious charge of assaulting a police officer.

After a night in the cells, she was charged and bailed to appear in court. I couldn't understand why she was so certain she was going to jail. But it turned out she had previous convictions I knew nothing about, and she was right to be afraid. The magistrate gave her two months in Holloway. It wasn't hard time and she only spent four weeks behind bars, but she was somehow different when she returned home. More distant and moody

I was so pleased to have her back that I put it down to 'jailhouse blues'. And I had some exciting news. While she was away I'd passed my driving test at the third attempt. Naïvely, I hoped it would help my job prospects and get me off the dole. Diane didn't share my pleasure. It may have been because this made me more independent. I was no longer reliant on her to drive me.

It also brought out the crazies. Someone must have seen me driving and targeted the car. They tried to set fire to it, but couldn't get the petrol cap off, so they smashed the rear window instead and scratched the paintwork.

Diane was furious and frightened. She took to staying in bed most of the day, or lying on the couch wrapped up in a blanket, sullenly drinking.

It was a miserable spring, and I'd have much worse to face up to. It turned out that Di had found another man – a rapist nearing the end of his sentence. And I had introduced them to each other. He was someone I'd met while on remand, and we had become sort of pals. I never knew what he was inside for.

After my release we kept in touch by phone and letter and I visited him once with Diane. I even bought him a guitar. If I'd known he was a rapist I wouldn't have allowed her anywhere near him. But he was a good-looking bloke and, unknown to me, Di was becoming obsessed with him. She wrote to him and had secret phone conversations, often from a public phone at the local supermarket.

I only became suspicious when I caught her speaking intimately on the phone to him from our bedroom. There were a series of blazing rows and within days she had packed her bags and moved in with his mother down at Epsom, to await his release.

Humiliation and rage ate me up. It was bad enough losing her to another man. But to a filthy rapist! That was too much. And, of course, the papers picked up the story to add to my indignity.

I suppose in truth she had become bored with me. Her experience of men in her past had been brutal and violent. Meek and mild me was too tame for her. Media interest, and the money it sometimes brought, had lost its appeal and become something of a pain. As Mrs Stagg, she found herself a target. Gary Howe seemed to offer a new and safer excitement for her, even with his record as a sex criminal.

If that was her hope it didn't last long. Drunken antics didn't go down well with his relatives. His mother had the cheek to phone me to complain about Diane, lying comatose drunk in their bathroom. It couldn't last. Within days, her rapist boyfriend decided she was no homecoming gift and ditched her from prison. She soon turned up, back on my doorstep – with a proposition!

If I was prepared to take the truth drug test to prove my innocence, she would come home to me. The incentive was the £20,000 she had been offered by the *News of the World*. With a big payday in mind she had contacted the crime reporter who'd written that big exclusive on my release. The paper jumped at the chance to give me the needle!

It was a difficult decision because I had a really deep dislike of drugs and injections. But on the plus side, it might help clear me in the public's mind, after all the recent bad publicity, and to end the 'Hate Stagg' campaign. The money was also a big incentive. So, despite my reservations about the test and my suspicion of Diane's motives, I agreed.

It was a disaster. Although the drug proved I hadn't murdered

Rachel, it showed up a small discrepancy about the timing of my visits to Wimbledon Common that day. The paper claimed this meant I'd lied to the police, and used this excuse not to pay us a penny. Diane was furious and blamed me. It was the end of the road.

We staggered on together at first, trying to play happy families for a few more weeks, but it was useless. I tried to encourage her to find work. After all, she was a trained health care worker, and it would give her pride and a sense of achievement. She wasn't interested. "I've worked for seven years and I've no intention of ever working again. You should have had money," was her less than loving reply.

The end was in sight, a few months short of both our third year together and our second wedding anniversary. I had made up my mind. If she left again she would never be allowed back. I couldn't take any more of her toying with my emotions.

The day it happened she was stretched out on the couch, all sullen and miserable, when she started having a go at me. "I ain't going to do this anymore. I'm leaving! I want a divorce and half of everything you own," she told me.

I told her she wasn't taking anything of mine, but she could go whenever she liked. With that she went upstairs, and I cooked lunch.

After coming down for her food, she had a few drinks and started another row. I couldn't stand it and took the dogs for a walk. When I returned there were two police officers – a man and a woman in the flat. Di had called them because she was "being held prisoner" and wanted to leave me. They could see it was ludicrous, but one of them helped her pack while I stayed in the sitting room.

We didn't say a word to each other. There were no goodbyes. The police drove her off to a women's refuge. That was the last I ever saw of her. But it wasn't to be the last I heard.

It was a strange feeling, being truly on my own at last. In the first couple of years I'd come to rely on her being there. It was us against the world, and I was devastated the first couple of times she left. But over the previous six months I'd come to terms with being alone again. And I'd faced the hatred of strangers by myself before. It still scared me, but I could cope. By now her departure was a relief.

My peace and quiet was short-lived though. With perfect timing, my old enemy the *Mail on Sunday* struck again in the wake of my domestic breakdown. On this occasion, their 'attack dog' was the hardline former Home Secretary, Norman Tebbit. He got on his soapbox about the double jeopardy law that prevented "trying murderers twice", as he put it. His opinion column was scathing about me. In fact, what he wrote was outrageous, downright dangerous, so bad that I was terrified of repercussions from the crazy brigade.

A picture of me bare-chested, walking my Labrador dogs, accompanied the piece. It was taken on a hot day so I was carrying my singlet. Tebbitt seized on this: "Women should beware that Colin Stagg walks over Richmond Park. He is often seen wearing a dodgy looking singlet and walking his black Alsatian dogs." I was described as "potentially dangerous", Tebbit advising that I "should be watched closely" and adding, "Be on your guard Mr Stagg, you should know that someone is watching you."

This was an open invitation to vigilante action against me. If that wasn't enough he bemoaned the legal system under which those who were acquitted could not be retried "even if new evidence suggests the verdict is wrong". What new evidence was he suggesting? Every development in the case has been towards my innocence, not guilt.

I was still shaking from his attack when Diane popped up – for what I thought was a farewell payout – in the *Sunday Mirror*. It was a fantasy about the marriage break-up caused by my 'violent temper' and our constant rowing. She ranted on about how she had been a virtual prisoner, finally seeking safety in a women's refuge with the help of the police and changing her name.

It would have been laughable, if it wasn't for the fresh threat letters that it triggered. But things did quieten down after that. Over the next six months I slowly settled into the life of a recluse that I still enjoy. Living quietly beneath people's radar, yet always on my guard.

Within a month of Diane leaving I began divorce proceedings. But she had other plans for me. Early in 1998 I received some strange calls from a man asking for Diane. I would tell him she didn't live here any more and put the phone down. On the fourth call he interrupted me to say, "I know she's not there. She's here with me and guess what I'm going to do to her?" He then went on to describe, in graphic detail, the sexual gymnastics they were going to perform on each other.

I listened with a sick sense of déjà vu. This was exactly what she had persuaded me to do to her ex-boyfriend after she left Milton Keynes to move in with me. I was determined not to let it affect me, but Diane had other ideas. She left a message with a neighbour asking me to phone her. Like an idiot I did, just as she had anticipated.

Instead of responding to my call, she let it go to answerphone. Without thinking, I left a message telling her, "Leave me alone" and adding, "You'll be dead by the third full moon if you don't stop calling this number."

That was just what she wanted. Armed with that tape she went to the police and the newspapers. The upshot was a three-page story in the *Sunday Express*, under the headline, 'STAGG TOLD ME: I KILLED RACHEL'. And I was later charged with making a threatening phone call.

Among the false and ridiculous claims made in the story was that "Diane is a calmer person than the one who regularly abused callers to the flat she shared with Stagg." Everyone on the estate got a good laugh out of that. There was little else to laugh at. She told a series of deliberately malicious lies that the newspaper never offered me a chance to refute.

A rumoured £10,000 fee helped revise our history, to give her both a payday and a payback. I'm convinced that our impending divorce played its part. The decree nisi came through only four days later. She was laughing at me all the way to the bank, showing how she could still earn money from our marriage.

Interestingly, even the usually hostile Fleet Street didn't give much credence to the story. I had expected to be besieged by hordes of reporters and cameramen, but nobody came and there were no-follow up stories the next day. The cynical hack-pack obviously thought Diane's story full of holes and decided to leave well alone.

But it still always seemed to be open season on Stagg. Newspapers could say what they liked about me without fear of retribution. A classic example of this happened a few months later. I had been taking my usual early morning walk with the dogs through Richmond Park, when I was attacked by a stag that slightly gored my leg.

The *Sunday People* got hold of what was admittedly –given my surname – quite an amusing little story. They did it up under the headline, 'Good news. Colin Stagg attacked by wild stag. Bad news. He is not badly hurt."

This sort of meanness and reluctance to say a kind word about me has become commonplace down the years. I am always "the prime suspect who was cleared of the Rachel Nickell murder" – or "cleared by a judge", implying that a jury would have given a very different verdict. They probably would have done. But that's not the point. Every time snide words like kinky, pervert, sex offender, weirdo, loner, misfit or jobless were used they reinforced a false public perception; whether it was as some sort of psychopath who got away with murder, or merely a nasty little lowlife who didn't deserve any sympathy. They helped to foster a climate of fear for me. That year, 1998, had been a public relations nightmare. (My only champion down the years has been *Private Eye*, and their columnist Paul Foot, who never stopped believing in my innocence.) And the Fourth Estate hadn't finished with me yet.

You would also think I'd have learned my lesson when it came to women who miraculously regarded me as a sex god. But call it lust or loneliness, I always lapped up their attention, however strangely it was packaged.

Nobody came more mysteriously wrapped than the girl I nicknamed 'the Blackbird', because she only came out at night. She fluttered into my nest by letter, as usual, pushed, not posted, through my door. It was another case of "I've seen you around the estate and I'd like to get to know you more." It was even probably a tabloid honeytrap. But I didn't care.

There hadn't been a woman in my bed for months, and this one had a lovely accent when I called her mobile. She also had nice handwriting. We agreed to meet for a drive a few days later. So, late one October afternoon, this exotic dusky maiden arrived at my door, bringing with her the flavour of the East.

Her skin was a warm brown and her perfume was musky. She had gleaming teeth, a lovely smile, long painted nails and a curvy figure. In short, she was sex on legs. I couldn't believe my luck.

We drove over to a quiet spot in nearby Richmond Park and pulled up. A lot happened in very short order. She confessed that, although she'd signed the letter as Kaitlynn, it wasn't her real name. I should call her Chemaine.

Her true identity had to be kept a secret, because she didn't want her wealthy family back in Mauritius to know she was involved with someone as notorious like me. Cheeky cow! But I quickly forgave her when she pulled me onto the back seat and bonked my brains out.

After dark we drove back to my place and went to bed for more fun and games. She left in the early hours and I promised to phone her. I was still no wiser about who she really was, where she lived or what she did for a living.

Over the next three weeks, she visited the flat for enthusiastic sex sessions but, at her insistence, only late at night. And she always wanted my assurance that I was alone when I phoned her. She sent me loving letters promising to look after me "emotionally, financially and sexually". I was a "very interesting guy" with whom she wanted a "caring and loving" relationship.

But something wasn't right. Although she claimed to work as a car saleswoman, I got the impression that she'd been stalking me during the day. She let slip things about people coming to my home, and where I'd been. She was supposed to be staying on the estate with some friends but wouldn't tell me exactly where. She had three mobiles but only gave me one number. Everything was moving too fast and she was setting the pace.

We only went out together once more, at her request for a midnight drive. After parking on Sheen Common we stripped off in the pitch dark and made love on a bench beside the woods. That wasn't enough for her. Now she wanted to do it in the woods, and suddenly ran off through the trees, stark naked, calling for me to follow her.

It was too cold and this didn't feel right. I got dressed instead and, while waiting for her to come back, decided I'd had enough of a good thing. I confided in the only media person I trusted. After describing her kinky sexual habits and how she'd contacted me, I happened to mention that she had three phones. He laughed out loud. "She's a pro, you idiot! Didn't you realise?"

I was horrified. It was obviously a set-up. 'Stagg Hooked By Hooker'. I could see the headline. For once, I agreed with the suggestion that I should go to the press. Giving out harmless stuff about a new girlfriend should defuse whatever she was planning. I was getting in the first strike.

After a lot of persuasion she agreed to an afternoon visit, and a photographer got shots of us together. From then on I ignored her phone calls and letters. It seemed to work. *The People* carried a lovey-dovey story, without the sex stuff, and it all went quiet.

Until the last Sunday of the year, when the 'Screws' printed their 'Weirdo Stagg's Sick Lust In Rachel Murder Woods!' nonsense. That was a tissue of lies about me forcing her to take part in a 'perverse' sex ritual near the murder scene, and how she had become terrified for her life. I hadn't been on the common since that fight by the pond. My dogs' walks were always in Richmond Park, and all the sexual demands were hers.

The rest of her story was a fiction involving, fear, danger, kinky sex demands and threats to her and her family. The only truth in it was the admission that she 'had been' an escort girl. Obviously, she'd been forced to invent the juicy bits on the premise that Stagg couldn't sue. Which was true enough – my solicitor said there was no hope of redress.

There and then, I vowed that never again would a woman who writes to me be allowed into my life. I had lived like a monk before, and I could do it again.

The first thing I did was sell the marital bed and all the bed linen. It wasn't for symbolism, I needed the cash. From then on I would share the couch with the dogs, or use my old sleeping bag. I didn't plan to share that with anyone.

Women and sex had brought me nothing but grief. I had one

rock-solid female friend I could rely on to always tell me the trut,h and believe in me. Sex, lies and letters would belong to the past. Or so I thought.

In many respects the next four years were worse than any prison sentence. The betrayals by Diane and this Kaitlynn woman hit me a lot harder than I wanted to admit. I thought I could overcome the emotional humiliation and tough it out. It proved a lot harder than I thought. Those were the bleakest years of my life. They culminated in that 'dark night of the soul' when I was seriously tempted to end it all. If I'm honest, I think I was suffering from clinical depression and should have sought professional help.

But I couldn't go to the doctor for fear it would leak out and get in the papers. Then it would look as if I was a nutter. For the same reason, I refused to visit the doctor for minor ailments. I would rather soldier on in pain or discomfort than expose myself to public scrutiny in the surgery. I can't bear the thought of people gossiping about what's wrong with me – it would only be lies.

The fear of violence against me never went away either. Nor the sense of being an outcast. If anything, my mental state has grown worse. Time would pass without incident and I would be lulled into a false sense of security. Then suddenly, complete strangers would make some disparaging remarks, or I'd be threatened, and it would all kick off again in my head.

I had hoped that, as time went by, people would forget about me or soften their attitude. This didn't happen. So I settled into a routine, not unlike the prison regimen that helped me to survive. It was much like being on a segregated wing. I tried to avoid human contact as much as possible. My day would start by taking the dogs for a very early walk in nearby Richmond Park, so as to avoid meeting people.

The majority who were about at that time of day were dog owners, and I felt safer because there is a sort of bond between animal lovers. Mostly this held true. There have been odd incidents, but the only occasion I was hurt was when a rutting stagg attacked me. (Gored by one of my namesakes!)

After my walk I would take the dogs home and have breakfast, then settle down in my 'cell'. There were no guards but I wouldn't go out again until after dark, to give my pets another run when no one could see me. It seems pathetic, but there were sound reasons for my behaviour. I kept off people's radar and avoided trouble. For I was always apprehensive whenever I went out.

My life became even more solitary. With the exception of Lee very few people visited me. I gave them no encouragement. My phone was cut off, which left me even more isolated. That was a parting gift from Diane. In the month before leaving she had run up a £400 bill, talking at length on a daily basis to the Runes (a sort of New Age fortune-telling phone line charged at premium rates).

Lee had been kind enough to lend me some money to buy a cheap run-around, but I could barely afford the maintenance and running costs. I only used it to take the dogs the few miles to Richmond Park. Money had become a real problem. All the luxury items bought in the early days after my release had been sold. Apart from a couple of personal items, anything of value had all gone. Even my treasured guitar. Luckily, I don't feel the cold badly so heating became a low priority. I had the gas supply disconnected and electricity put on a coin meter.

Those years around the new millennium were a sort of hibernation period. I eked out a subsistence level existence, trying to remain unnoticed. That was my priority. Lying low. The nights were worst. I didn't sleep well, and was plagued by dreams. Some of them were disturbing and frightening. Even my subconscious believed people were out to get me.

The slightest unfamiliar sound would wake me. I'd wander round the flat at 3am, checking the doors and windows to make sure nobody had broken in. I was living in a climate of fear. Everyone's hand seemed turned against me and I was always on my guard, whenever I ventured out. In some respects, merely being recognised was worse than threats or name-calling. I realised how much I hated being stared at by strangers. To this day I hate seeing that look of recognition on their faces.

Back in 2002, I took a short break for two or three days on the Welsh borders. In the middle of nowhere, I stopped at a cottage to ask directions. Before I could speak, the owner looked at me and said, "I know you from somewhere. Your face is so familiar. Do you live in the next village?" I guess it's like that for celebrities – only in my case, nobody will want autographs. And as a strange kind of celebrity, I also acquired my own stalker.

Her name was Shannon and she dogged me for eight years, until I finally had to obtain a court order to stop her pestering me. I never knew anything about her except that she lived in north London with her mum. On her first appearance, shortly before Diane finally moved out, she got into the flat by saying she was my cousin. I had never seen her in my life, but she seemed harmless enough, so we let her stay and gave her some tea.

Months later she turned up on my doorstep. It was the dead heart of winter and she was turning blue with cold, so again I invited her in. She was a skinny young thing dressed in a jacket and mini-skirt, and it soon became obvious she was obsessed by me. I got rid of her as soon as possible.

But over the years she kept coming back, making a nuisance of herself. She sent me long, rambling letters saying we were made for each other, or scrawled loving messages on my door in lipstick. Sometimes she would appear in the street outside. I tried to ignore her in the hope she would eventually give up.

But it got worse. She persuaded a Sunday newspaper we'd had an affair and that she was pregnant by me. They believed her until a simple pregnancy test proved it was nonsense. That didn't deter her. Soon afterwards, she turned up one night with a curry and an overnight bag hoping to stay. I sent her packing. But she kept coming back when I least expected it.

It got so bad I had an old video camera positioned outside and linked to my TV, so I could see who was at the door. Strangers and Shannon were not welcome. I *did* make one exception for a lady who lived nearby. She was married, in her late forties and we had been on nodding terms for years.

We got chatting at the supermarket counter one day and I invited her back for coffee. One thing led to another and we became occasional lovers. Months would go by sometimes, until she fancied an afternoon sex session. That was fine by me. There were no strings attached and I could trust her not to go to the papers. And I liked her.

The only other woman who briefly entered my life during those barren years was Bernie. She turned up after an analysis of DNA material seemed to clear me. This tall, attractive blonde was about my age and lived on the estate. She called round one evening while my uncle Tony was visiting. We stayed in the kitchen, talking easily for a bit, and she agreed to return later when he had gone. But she never turned up and I went to bed, only to be awakened by a 2am phone call.

It seems she had lost her nerve earlier but wanted to see me there and then. I was a bit groggy, and there were bad memories of 'the Blackbird', but I thought, "What the hell? I don't get offers like this every night." She did seem very keen.

And she was. Spectacularly so! I couldn't believe my luck. But our affair only lasted a few more weeks before she moved away.

These were my only sexual experiences in what I think of as the barren years, and they weren't what you would call 'relationships'. I did have Lee's friendship to sustain me, and she tried to ensure that both me and the dogs at least had enough to eat when the bills overwhelmed me.

She even tried to find work for me, but employers didn't want to know. I applied for a job as a meter reader after they had promised her that they would ignore the newspaper lies. I passed their first interview, and then nothing. No explanation. No rejection. No job offer. That's what it's been like ever since the trial.

Is it any wonder I have such a low opinion of the police and what they have done to me?

THIRTEEN

If anyone detests the Metropolitan Police hierarchy more than me it's ex-Detective Inspector Keith Pedder. He has good reason to.

By an incredible twist of fate they put him through an ordeal that almost exactly paralleled mine, and he learned first-hand what it's like to be wrongly accused. He became the victim of a flawed 'sting' operation and spent a night in the cells before being bailed. It took another agonising nine months before he was charged with a crime he did not commit.

He was sent for trial at the Old Bailey, with the shadow of disgrace and a hefty jail sentence hanging over him for an alleged conspiracy to corrupt a police officer. If he'd been convicted, he would have done hard time. The newspapers gleefully reported his apparent fall from grace. Work dried up and the strain on his home life took its toll on his health.

Luckily for him, when he appeared at the Bailey another judge dismissed the undercover evidence as unsafe and he was acquitted. But the damage was done. As with me, the stigma has followed him to this day. As a detective with twenty years' experience, much of it with elite squads, he could have expected a top job in the private sector.

But the Chinese whispers about his integrity somehow spread into big business. He sailed through high-powered job interviews only to be rejected for the post. He has been forced to take work well below his capabilities, leaving him understandably bitter. It only makes me think of my own 'unemployable' tag.

His disenchantment with certain senior ranks of the Met grew in the aftermath of my acquittal. In his view they scrambled to distance themselves from the undercover operation they so enthusiastically condoned and actively authorised. The lower ranks were left to carry the burden left by the failure of the £3million Nickell murder inquiry. He didn't return to operational duties.

Instead he was moved to SO11 at Scotland Yard where he worked on intelligence gathering. His career was stalled, despite the attempts of several senior officers to protect him from the fallout. The stress led to health problems and, fifteen months after I walked out of the Central Criminal Court, he handed his papers in and said goodbye to 'the Job'. He was only thirty-nine.

After his resignation it became known in police circles that he planned to write a warts-and-all book about the whole Rachel Nickell investigation. As a civilian he would be free to reveal the true involvement of senior police and CPS staff in Operation Edzell and its repercussions.

He had copied the docket that set out exactly who sanctioned it, and how far up the chain of command they were. The names included two Deputy Assistant Commissioners, two Commanders, two Detective Chief Superintendents, several Detective Chief Inspectors and numerous Met police solicitors.

That wasn't calculated to win him applause from the big boys in blue. It was just his bad luck that he gave them a perfect chance to neutralise him in March 1998. While working as a security consultant, he recognised what appeared to be police surveillance on the man he was targeting.

Anxious not to compromise an operation, he asked an old friend (still a serving officer) to check if this case was flagged on the operations register. He was also concerned for his own safety, in case it turned out that the suspect was a violent criminal. His isolated observation point made him vulnerable.

But the detective constable suspected he was being set up himself and, to cover his back, reported the approach to his superiors. The Yard's Complaints and Investigations Bureau couldn't believe their luck. High-level approval was given for a 'sting' operation to trap the man who was thought to be rocking the force's boat.

A pub meeting was arranged by the contact near Pedder's home. But he smelled a rat when the man arrived with an envelope containing microfiche records taken off the Police National Computer. This was not what had been asked for. Pedder had merely looked for guidance in what he had thought was a responsible way. He grew even more uncomfortable when his old friend made the universal sign for money by rubbing his finger and thumb together.

Pedder pointed out that money had never previously been discussed, or even considered. At that the officer walked off, leaving the envelope lying on the table. Pedder says there was no question of letting it stay there in a crowded pub, so he picked it up. Undercover officers immediately pounced.

Until that moment he had committed no crime. Now, it seemed, they had him bang to rights. He was arrested for alleged corruption and spent the night in the cells at his local police station, before being released on bail.

Meanwhile CIB officers raided his home and seized documents and, most tellingly, searched high and low for his computer. They didn't find it. He was by now convinced they were looking for his manuscript. This seems borne out by comments made to him by the duty solicitor at Bromley Police Station, when he was eventually allowed access to legal representation. (He has described this delay as "an illegal act designed to deprive me of legal advice.")

When the solicitor, whom he had never met before, walked into his cell, he said, "My goodness, Mr Pedder, they seem to regard you as a very big fish, but they are more concerned about a book you may have written. I heard the officers talking about it before I came in."

Nine agonising months later, he was formally charged. When I first heard the news of his arrest, I must admit I was pleased. He was going to find out firsthand what I had endured. But as time passed, the more I thought about it the less likely it seemed. This man had never done me any favours. He had pursued me relentlessly, blighted my life and caused me a lot of harm. All the same, there didn't actually seem to be anything corrupt about him. Pedder would never bend the rules, like some of them, and you couldn't ever imagine him crossing the line. I never dreamed that he would end up, like me, at the Old Bailey.

But the judge threw out the CIB evidence as unsafe and acquitted him finally in September 1999. Justice seemed to have been done. Although I was still glad he'd been given a taste of his own medicine.

Despite being treated like a criminal, Pedder tells us he remains fiercely loyal to the force – if not its leaders: "I am extremely supportive of the Metropolitan Police Service and always will be. I only have issues with the behaviour of small cadres of senior officers." Time hasn't changed his view of the Nickell case very much either – he is still prickly at what he sees as unjust condemnation of the whole investigation, including the honeytrap operation.

But, in the interests of what he saw as bringing balance to my story, he agreed to give an interview to my collaborator, veteran journalist Ted Hynds. The two of them had first met (like us) via TV's *The Cook Report* and become friends. (They also attended the same school, nearly twenty years apart. Its motto was 'God's Gift'!) Like me, he trusted Ted enough to give a frank appraisal of Rachel's murder and its aftermath. He made some surprising criticisms of both Britton and a section of the Met hierarchy.

And he still has reservations about me, but tempers his earlier conviction that I was the killer. As he admits now, "I do feel sorry for Colin Stagg. He has paid a terrible price for a man found not guilty of murder after due process of law. The press campaign against him has been relentless and unjust.

"But I don't believe he has a justifiable complaint against the handling of the murder inquiry. Our job was only to deliver evidence, not judgement. The case was brought to trial by the Crown Prosecution Service. Nobody else.

"They were consulted on the legality of the undercover operation from its inception. Their approval was fundamental and at no time did they ever express doubts about Operation Edzell's implementation.

"Mr Stagg's second arrest in August 1993 was carried out with their blessing. But they merely gave us permission to charge him with murder. They proceeded with the prosecution. The police had lost the power to bring prosecutions a decade earlier.

"He was then held on remand for thirteen months. A stipendiary magistrate committed him for an Old Bailey Trial after a contested eleven-day old-style committal. The case itself was on the Attorney General's 'most sensitive' list for nine months and regularly updated.

"Nowhere along this timeline was our evidence queried. There was ample opportunity for them to withdraw the charge. If the police were that wrong in law, what was the case doing at the Old Bailey?

"Even after the Not Guilty result the DPP (Director of Public Prosecutions) Barbara Mills sent out a memo telling her staff to 'pay no attention' to what the press say. According to her, it was 'a prosecution that was rightfully brought, so don't listen to the media.'

"That doesn't sound like someone having second thoughts. Yet a liberal judge reserved his most scathing condemnation for the police and the psychologist who assisted them. He made no mention of the pivotal role played by the CPS in deciding to bring the case to trial.

"It should also be noted that the legality of the covert op was overseen throughout by a very senior CPS prosecutor, Howard Youngerwood

"Only a few months before Stagg was indicted he took the decision to drop charges against some of the Eltham Five in the high-profile Stephen Lawrence murder case.

"That was one of the most sensitive and potentially explosive cases of the decade, yet he still made the difficult and controversial decision to withdraw. If the Stagg case was so fatally flawed, why didn't he do the same in that instance?"

I understand what Pedder says about the CPS – but I should never have been charged on that so-called 'evidence', let alone sent to the Old Bailey for trial. And it was Paul Britton's flawed psychological reading of my personality that provided the basis for it.

I didn't go looking for Lizzie James, she came to me. I only responded to what I thought she wanted. Looking back at those letters of hers, it's clear I was manipulated. And that was *all* they had to go on.

Perhaps not surprisingly, Keith Pedder doesn't agree:

"At the outset Colin focused attention on himself by his odd behaviour immediately after the murder, and by the discrepancies in his timings for visits to the common that morning. The evidence of Susan Gale was crucial in this respect. Mr Stagg claimed she got her dates mixed up and suggested their meeting was some days later. But her husband wouldn't let her go back on the common after the murder.

"Her mother-in-law also confirmed she had asked to be taken home early to collect her pension on the day of the murder. Details from the pension book backed this up. We spent a lot of time checking this out.

"Then there was his meeting with PC Crouch by the underpass. Time of death had not been established by then, yet Mr Stagg was keen to put himself at home during the relevant time – which was at odds with Mrs Gale's evidence. It suggested that he knew how important that timing would prove to be.

"His strange story about meeting a couple on his first visit to the common – a woman with a buggy and a 'miserable git' who ignored his 'good morning' – raised doubts. This pair were never traced despite extensive inquiries.

"What also stood out was his unusually excited behaviour with Pat Heanen, the butcher, and newsagent Patel, and his meeting with the old lady Lillian Avid. All this from a man who didn't normally say boo to a goose.

"From being someone who is only on the periphery of people's awareness, all of a sudden he is the centre of attention, talking away very excitedly, about a subject he shouldn't know so much about.

"He had lied to us about the crucial times he had been on the common. The TV programme he claimed to have watched had not been aired that day.

"His general behaviour was suspicious. He was doing and saying things that didn't stack up. This combination made us focus attention upon him. What else were we to do?

"We had to ask ourselves, 'What is this person telling us? Does it hold up?' And once we looked at these discrepancies, as they started to unfurl, he moved from being a witness to becoming a potential suspect.

"The evidence of Jane Harriman was crucial in this respect. She had described the man she had observed acting suspiciously near the murder scene as having a distinctive walk, and had later identified that man as Stagg in an identity parade.

"After his indecent exposure hearing he was filmed on TV, hurrying away from Wimbledon Magistrates' Court. Immediately afterwards she phoned us with important news.

"Mrs Harriman said she had been one hundred per cent sure after the ID parade. But now she had seen him walking, and instantly recognised his strange gait, she was one hundred and twenty per cent sure. This was the same man she had seen on the common.

"It was extremely important. Her sighting had already conformed to the required Turnbull criteria – named after a famous case which set the standards for identification of suspects in regards to light, view, distance and angle to the subject.

"Although we had just about enough to charge him there was nowhere near the evidence needed to secure a conviction. The motive was almost certainly sexual, but we had no link to our suspect.

"It was the worst time in any murder hunt. Dozens of potential suspects had been interviewed, hundreds of leads followed up and statements taken. But we had got nowhere.

"There was no forensic evidence, no murder weapon, no eyewitness except for a little boy one month short of his third birthday. We had reached an impasse."

I can understand Keith Pedder's frustrations. Even now, despite what I endured at their hands, I'm not so biased that I can't sympathise with the problems faced by the murder squad.

It was my bad luck that I turned up at the wrong time. They were desperate for someone to home in on, and I fell into their lap. If I had become a suspect within days of the murder, I think I would have been off the hook. The clothes I wore that day would have been unwashed, though they would still have been able to run forensic checks and find no evidence, as washing doesn't eradicate blood completely. People's memories would also have been much clearer, including mine.

Two months later, I wasn't exactly sure what time I got back to the flat. I wasn't clear what had been showing on the TV when I lay down on the couch. And I maintain that Susan Gale got her dates mixed up. As for the Jane Harriman identification, the photofit she produced for *Crimewatch* was an identical match for the murderer whom DNA evidence has clearly made him the prime suspect for Rachel's killing.

It was the combination of Britton's profiling and Pedder's determination to catch this killer at all costs that led them down the undercover path. Pedder and I may not like each other very much, but I've come to realise there was nothing personal in his fixation on me.

He was following what he considered a valid chain of evidence. That it was *wrong* didn't help me at the time though. It is now generally accepted that the Lizzie James op was ill conceived. That was why she received her big compensation payout. But everyone, from the highest-ranking police officers to the head of the CPS, were carried away by the novelty of the idea. There was no 'safety net' in place to deal with the possible psychological damage to an innocent suspect, or even the undercover officer. It was put together in a hurry without proper safeguards.

Keith Pedder insists they were assured by independent advisors that there was no danger. But how would they know if an innocent suspect had been mentally damaged? They weren't going to tell him about the secret operation, so they couldn't carry out any examination or offer counselling afterwards. I was never offered treatment.

And if they had revealed the deception that was more likely to cause mental anguish, it would almost certainly give grounds to bring a massive damages action. Too much reliance was placed on the conclusions that Paul Britton drew from its results – which is why it was thrown out by the judge.

I was encouraged into expressing wilder and wilder fantasies every step of the way, which were then used against me as 'proof' that I was a murderer. It was treated as hard evidence, not fantasy.

Obviously Mr Pedder has a very different view.

"A lot of careful consideration went into this operation. Paul Britton designed it on what was known of the killer – along the lines, 'Because he has done this we can say this about him.' It was not specifically aimed at Colin Stagg.

"We had a responsibility to find the right person, before he killed again. There would be a series of psychological ladders for a suspect to climb and only the killer would mount them.

"If he didn't he would eliminate himself. This was how I understood it in layman's terms. Of course there was a risk assessment, or we wouldn't have been allowed to go ahead.

"Advice was taken from other psychologists and we were told there was no danger of any mental damage to an innocent suspect.

"There was a disengagement policy whereby, if the suspect eliminated himself, Lizzie would take two or three weeks to gently cool things and bring the relationship to an end by taking a job abroad.

"The real fear was, regarding Paul Britton's conclusion, that the killer would inevitably strike again. We were worried that if we engaged with the killer it might prompt an action he might otherwise not have taken. He might murder sooner rather than later.

"We watched over months with growing conviction as Colin Stagg climbed the psychological ladders. For me the key moment occurred at the end of their first meeting in Hyde Park.

"He handed Lizzie a fantasy letter, KP35 in the evidence list. Critically it had been written before their meeting and introduced the use of a knife for sexual pleasure, just as Paul Britton had predicted.

"From there his fantasies moved on involving blood and violence. The operation might have lasted a lot longer than first predicted, but it seemed to have been a success. The CPS certainly thought so."

That was the trouble. They all thought wrong. It took a sensible judge to see how I had been manipulated and how flimsy the case against me was.

The verdict was a career-breaking blow for Pedder. He never recovered from the fallout. Sidelined from major investigation and with promotion prospects zero, he suffered depression and took voluntary retirement fifteen months later. Like me, he is understandably bitter at his treatment.

Pedder: "The covert operation was authorised from the highest levels of the Met and only then did we put it into practice.

"In the aftermath of the trial collapse most of the high ranking officers involved went on to bigger and better things.

"Deputy Assistant Commissioner Ian Johnston, who authorised the operation, was promoted to Assistant Commissioner. He has since gone on to become a Chief Constable in the British Transport Police. Those of us at the bottom of the chain were treated as an embarrassment.

"The irony didn't escape us when Mr Johnston was appointed to head an inquiry 'into the conduct' of the whole investigation, including the covert op he had authorised.

"His inquiry had been set up within a week by the Commissioner, Sir Paul Condon, after parliamentary pressure for a thorough review. It didn't focus on what happened to the troops.

"The treatment of Lizzie James was disgusting. She was one of the bravest officers I ever met, who took on this stressful operation within three months of getting married.

"On her return to SO10, where she had been one of their star undercover operators, she was hung out to dry.

"She was only given routine work and she started getting flak from her bosses. A series of appalling appraisal reports made it clear that her career was over.

"The stress pushed her to the edge and affected her health. She went on sick leave and the Police Federation began a civil action on her behalf against the Met. They settled on the court steps eighteen months later.

"Her solicitors issued a statement afterward saying, 'The willingness of the Metropolitan Police to pay substantial damages must indicate their recognition that she sustained serious psychiatric injury.'

"What hacks me off is the shabby way the whole team was treated for doing their jobs to the best of their abilities. The thoroughness of the murder investigation could not be faulted.

"These fifty-six officers worked thousands of hours of unpaid overtime to tackle the immense workload. This murder touched each one of them deeply. Above all they were dedicated to finding justice for Rachel."

Unlike me, Pedder had the advantage of a strong family foundation and he was able to rebuild his life. I'm still waiting for the new DNA evidence to result in a formal charge. It will take that to finally clear me in the public's mind.

But Pedder isn't so sure:

"After this length of time there is always a chance that the integrity of the exhibit, on which it was found, has been compromised.

"You have to satisfy yourselves that the golden thread of continuity has not been broken. I'm unsure whether that can be safely said here, in light of the gigantic advances made in respect of the sensitivity of the DNA science that is now available.

"There were three post-mortems carried out on Rachel and each time the case was reviewed her clothing would have been re-examined and been open to contamination.

"The same applies when the sample is matched against that of the new suspect. All these things are carried out in the same lab and it is always possible for secondary transfer to occur.

"I think it better to withhold judgement until the CPS decides whether or not to charge this man. Even though he is a Broadmoor patient he could still be charged and then deemed unfit to plead. As usual it's up to the CPS, not the police.

"In the meantime I wish Colin well. He has had years of bad press despite being acquitted and the law saying he didn't do it. I will keep an open mind on the subject of the new forensic evidence for the moment.

"I feel more sorry for the Nickell family. I don't think they have been served well. They deserve some form of closure to this tragedy."

He's quite right. The Nickells, Andre Hanscombe, and most of all Alex – now reputedly a troubled teenager – must have hoped they would be able to put this horror behind them by now. But I don't suppose they ever will.

Nor will I. Strangely enough, in our different ways, I think we are all missing the same thing. Justice. I'm luckier, because I only want justice for a ruined life, which can at least be rebuilt. They need it for a life that was horribly snatched from them forever. Nothing can ever compensate for that.

Their suffering is so much harder to bear, and it also requires someone to blame. The face of the killer. An individual to project their anger and terrible sense of loss at. For lack of anyone else to focus on, that person has been me. They wanted, *needed*, someone to pay for this. I suspect they would have preferred me to go down for murder even if I was freed later on appeal. As it turned out, they were left in limbo for fourteen years. The judge's ruling left them feeling cheated

Despite their dignified behaviour and very rare interviews, the Nickells have made it clear they believe I was the likely killer. That's all they've had to hang onto. Andrew Nickell's thinly veiled accusation on the Old Bailey steps, when he called for justice for his daughter, is proof of that. He felt betrayed by the law he had put his faith in.

Andre Hanscombe lost his lover, the mother of his child. He has never bothered to disguise his hatred of me. I've always been guilty in his eyes and probably always will be.

So I've tried to make allowances for their tragic loss, and the grief they must still be enduring. But how much easier for them to accept the unofficial Met line that I got off on a technicality.

Nobody can blame them, after all the anti-Stagg propaganda they must have seen. I've been portrayed as the despicable scum of the earth, who doesn't deserve pity or sympathy, guilty or not. How did the *Daily Star* so impolitely put it? "A disgusting excuse for a man."

In the past four years there has been growing forensic evidence that I was innocent, as I have always insisted. Now a double killer and multiple rapist, caged in Broadmoor mental hospital, looks likely to be charged. As far as I'm concerned, the evidence has firmly established my innocence of this monstrous crime, even if the press has only grudgingly come round to that viewpoint.

An acknowledgement that I may have been wrongly accused of Rachel's murder would be nice. Something along those lines from her family would go a long way to removing my 'marked man' status. Perhaps a mere expression of regret at what's happened to me. Keith Pedder was decent enough to manage that, after all.

If their perceptions of me were different, I would have liked to personally express the sorrow I felt at Rachel's death. I would like to look them straight in the eye and have them know, once and for all, that I was not the monster who took their daughter from them.

That's a pipedream. They will probably take huge offence at the mere suggestion, coming as it does from me. They needed someone to pay. But as long as they continue to maintain their silence, the longer some people will continue to deny my innocence.

Over the past fifteen years I have had to endure every physical and verbal form of attack. I've had to swallow terrible insults, read the wildly inaccurate stories and downright lies written about me, all the while living in fear.

Any form of employment has been made impossible. A working class man with no work is left to exist on a state pittance. It's not in the same league as losing a daughter, but it's no picnic.

Try living like that for a decade and a half and you'll know what I mean.

But if I regret the Nickells' silence, I feel anger and resentment at the public body that has resolutely dismissed all attempts to clear my name. They owe me a big, big apology, and one day soon the Metropolitan Police Service may just have to give it to me. If they do it will have been dragged out of them. But I won't care, provided they acknowledge that what they did to me was wrong.

Perhaps I shouldn't hold my breath. Hard evidence that could have cleared me only surfaced publicly four years ago.

In a controlled leak to the *Daily Mail*, it was quietly revealed inside their Saturday edition that forensic experts had made a vital breakthrough. Using the DNA low-copy number technique, they recovered a minute sample of male DNA from Rachel's underwear, which in all probability came from her killer.

This revelation came fourteen months after the Yard launched its second review of the case, to coincide with the tenth anniversary of Rachel's death. The tiny speck of cellular material was only a 'partial sample', meaning it did not provide detectives with a full profile and identity of the killer. But most importantly for me, it was sufficient to eliminate potential suspects and family members. (It had already ruled out Andre and Alex.)

That left only the murderer who could have had such intimate contact with her body that day. All the detectives had to do was check it against the sample they'd taken from me at the time of my arrest. I'd be in the clear at last.

Yet it wasn't to be that simple. The *Mail* story suggested that my sample might have been destroyed after the acquittal. And then, in a classic example of Fleet Street putting the boot in, they added, "If Stagg refused any request to give a voluntary sample police would not automatically have the right to arrest him.

They would have to have additional grounds such as witness testimonies linking him to the murder."

It was a subtle hint that I might be reluctant to volunteer for a new test. *Reluctant!* Wild horses couldn't have stopped me giving a sample. But the Met did. Since that announcement in September 2003, they have stubbornly refused to allow me to take the ten-second test that would confirm my innocence.

Within days my solicitor, Alex Tribick, wrote to the Metropolitan Police Commissioner expressing my wish to volunteer a DNA test for the purpose of excluding me from the Nickell inquiry once and for all. It took almost a month for Britain's top cop to decline my offer. My new local MP, Tony Coleman, wasn't interested in helping either.

So in November of that year we tried Lord Harris of Harringay, the chairman of the Metropolitan Police Authority, with a view to gaining his assistance. A prompt acknowledgement was given, together with the promise of a further response "as soon as possible". Nothing more was ever heard from Lord Harris or the authority.

Mr Tribick refused to give up, and, in March 2004, he appeared to have won a breakthrough. He got in touch with the senior officer at Wimbledon Police Station, Detective Chief Inspector Harper. The DCI felt it was reasonable, under the circumstances, for an innocent man to have his DNA put on the national database in order to be excluded from a crime scene,

It was agreed that I should attend the station with my solicitor one morning, when appropriate samples would be taken. I thought I'd won the lottery!

But not for long. When we arrived for the test we were greeted by a rather embarrassed DCI, who took us into a side room where he explained that the Metropolitan Police were now refusing to take any samples from me for analysis. Obviously he had informed his superiors of the decision to take my DNA, and overnight they had stamped on the idea.

I was so despondent I turned to the press for help. *The Sun* organised a DNA test and tried to get the result accepted at Scotland Yard. It was only a publicity stunt to persuade the Met to agree to run tests on me themselves. And it failed. For their own reasons, the police didn't want to eliminate me. But they may now have to do so, thanks to the dedication and stubbornness of my solicitor.

Nobody has worked harder to rescue my good name than Alex Tribick. Thanks to his incredible tenacity, Colin Stagg may finally be on the verge of rehabilitation. This stocky, rugby-mad legal dynamo may have achieved the seemingly impossible: official acknowledgement that I was unfairly treated during the Nickell murder investigation. His relentless efforts, regularly firing off letters on my behalf, have resulted in an *ex gratia* ('without acknowledgement of blame') award from the Home Office. He had petitioned them for compensation for over two years, even after I felt it was hopeless.

Finally, on January 10th 2007, a letter – strangely dated December 8th 2006 – arrived at his law firm, W. H. Matthews in Staines, confirming my eligibility for payment under the Discretionary Compensation Scheme. Payouts are made following wrongful conviction or arrest "arising because of a serious default by a public authority or through exceptional circumstances such as complete exoneration".

It took me completely by surprise. So did the *Daily Mail*'s exclusive story about the award that same day. (They must have known about it before us!) It was more or less accurate, save for the most important fact. The headline stated I was to receive £250,000, which was totally wrong. The award, which is still in the process of being assessed, is not a specific figure. Wildly differing and totally inaccurate sums have been mentioned – but then, that's invariably been my experience with the media.

It is a sort of personal injury claim, in respect of lost earnings and psychological damage, plus pain and injury caused by public vilification. An independent lawyer is acting as the assessor of what I have lost, which has taken some seven months to compile. Extra time was granted because of the difficulty in obtaining one specific major requirement – a psychological report.

A significant number of psychologists were approached, and each of them had an excuse to turn down the job once it was revealed that Colin Stagg was their subject. One did finally accept the assignment, only to back out at the last minute because he feared he would lose patients if they discovered he was examining me!

The behaviour of these so-called professional men was so upsetting that I considered dropping the claim. Since my bitter experience at the hands of Paul Britton, psychologists are my least favourite people.

If ever the assessor required hard evidence of the unjust way I have been perceived and treated over fifteen years, this was it. Only the time and effort exerted by Alex on my behalf stopped me from pulling out. I owed him too much for fighting my corner when everybody else – including me – felt like giving up.

It was also a harsh fact that the press would have a field day. They wouldn't see my withdrawal as a matter of principle. Their headlines would be variations on 'Stagg Fears Award Scrutiny', or 'Stagg Compensation Claims Collapses'. The publicity backlash would inevitably have brought a fresh round of Stagg-bashing.

Common sense prevailed, and I calmed down. But this episode shows how, even today, my name alone is enough to cause even educated, professional people to rapidly distance themselves.

Alex's resolve to seek an award was triggered by an incredible discovery. In November 2004, it was revealed that the DNA sample found on Rachel's body had finally been matched.

It belonged to a vicious double killer and multiple rapist, currently held in Broadmoor secure mental hospital. Robert Clive Napper is a paranoid schizophrenic who was identified as the killer of a young mother and her little daughter, and a true sexual deviant.

After his arrest in May 1994, DNA evidence also revealed him to be the so-called 'Green Chain rapist'. Between 1986 and 1994, he had carried out over seventy savage rapes and serious sexual assaults along and around the miles of linked footpaths and parks known as Green Chain Walk in southeast London.

At the Old Bailey in October 1995, minutes before the jury was to decide if he was fit to stand trial, he changed his not guilty plea to guilty of manslaughter on the grounds of diminished responsibility. He also admitted two of the Green Chain rapes and two attempted rapes in 1992. Sentencing him, Mr Justice Hooper said he posed a "grave and immediate risk to the public" and ordered him to be detained "without time or limit". Napper, now forty-one, has been in Broadmoor ever since.

Detectives reviewing the Nickell case in 2002 wanted to interview Napper to check for possible links. Doctors refused permission because of his deteriorating mental condition. It wasn't until July 2006, well after the DNA identification, that they were able to spend two days with him. Early in 2007, it was leaked to the press that the CPS were preparing charges and he was likely to be indicted around Easter.

Like so many things relating to Rachel's murder, nothing more has been heard and an official silence has been maintained. Hopefully it may break soon.

New evidence has revealed that Napper received psychiatric treatment at a clinic close to Wimbledon Common.
We're told that the DNA sample matches him by odds of five million to one against it being someone else – and that, as of November 2007, he will be charged with Rachel's murder any day now.

FOURTEEN

O ne person who didn't stay silent in the light of the Napper revelation was Paul Britton. He rushed into print to rewrite history, by claiming the police had dismissed his advice, back in 1993, that the killer of Samantha Bissett and her child might also have been responsible for Rachel's murder. He went as far as to say that rape investigators could have prevented all three deaths, if they had followed his profiling advice years earlier.

And to cap it all, he tried to wriggle out of any responsibility for the Lizzie James fiasco. He asserted he had never thought the letters were a good idea and had questioned the legal basis for the covert operation. It was nonsense! You only had to turn to his own book, written in the previous decade, to measure his claims against his own words.

But he fooled the *Independent on Sunday* and their home affairs correspondent, Sophie Goodchild, into writing up this rubbish without first checking Britton's allegations. (Another example of Fleet Street's allergy to factual reporting.) Five days after the

Napper DNA find was announced, the paper ran a prominent story under the following headline: "Police ignored clues that could have led to Rachel Nickell's killer, says expert. *IoS* investigation: Three murders might have been prevented if psychological profile of serial attacker had been considered."

It went on: "Britain's leading criminal profiler advised detectives to investigate clues linking the murder of Rachel Nickell with the brutal killing of another young mother – but they dismissed any connection, *The Independent on Sunday* can reveal.

"The claim follows Scotland Yard's revelation that detectives believe one man – Robert Napper – may have been responsible for both the murder of Ms Nickell on Wimbledon Common in 1992 and the slaying of Samantha Bissett and her four year old daughter Jazmine nearly a year and a half later.

"Napper, who is detained indefinitely in Broadmoor, convicted of the Bissett murders, is also suspected of being the Green Chain rapist, who carried out at least seventy savage attacks across south-east London in a four-year spree more than ten years ago."

The story linked the similarities of these savage sexual attacks with the Nickell and Bissett murders, in which both young women were mutilated. It also revealed that detectives were awaiting clearance to question Napper as the new prime suspect, after his DNA was found on Rachel's underclothes.

The implications for me, and what had been done to me, were obvious.

Then their hero was revealed with a flourish. Paul Britton was introduced as the psychological profiler on whom the TV series *Cracker* was based. He told them, "Samantha Bissett would never have been killed if my early advice had been acted upon, and if it is the same person, then neither would Rachel Nickell."

After being brought in to assist on the Green Chain case, he told them, he had given the police three pointers which, he claimed, would lead them to the rapist. His belief was that the attacker would already be on their records for minor offences. He would have been noticed by neighbours, and his suspicious behaviour would have been mentioned at local police briefings. "To this day I do not understand why this did not happen," said Britton. "We were looking at an escalating offender. My advice was to look at the case from a local level."

Napper was finally arrested for the Bissett murders after his fingerprint was found on a rear balcony of their basement flat in Plumstead. He never admitted the Green Chain rapes.

Perhaps it was just coincidence, but I know now that Rachel had lived for months in Plumstead at the same time as Robert Napper was committing the Green Chain attacks. When she moved to Balham, after meeting Andre, they were still going on.

It may seem farfetched, but since Napper was put in the frame for her murder, I've had this niggling little thought in the back of my mind. Could he somehow have recognised her from her time in southeast London? It doesn't seem possible, but whatever the truth, it's still very strange.

Then the story switched to Wimbledon Common murder, describing how I became the focus of a Met sting operation by a female undercover officer. "Operating under the name Lizzie James, the officer wrote a series of sexually intimate letters to Mr Stagg. He never confessed but was charged – only for the case to be thrown out by a judge in 1993 on the grounds that the police had used entrapment.

"It had always been assumed that Mr Britton, who drew up a psychological profile for police of the Wimbledon Common killer, wrote the Lizzie James letters. But he revealed that this is not true and he also said that he questioned the legal basis for using a sting operation to extract a confession from Mr Stagg."

Britton was quoted as saying, "Not only did I not write them, but I did not see them until they had been sent. It was never my notional suggestion that it would be a good idea to write the letters."

I couldn't believe my eyes when I read this. It went on to say he had been exonerated in 2002 of any wrongdoing in the case after an eight-year inquiry by the British Psychological Society. Britton revealed he had examined fourteen hours of taped interviews with me and that the operation was presented to a 'top-level' police meeting where it was given full approval.

The next quote seemed to indicate Britton had been in attendance. "My first question was: 'Is this legal?' What the police said echoes forever: 'Please don't concern yourself with legal issues.'"

He continued: "This case was at the very top of the Attorney General's watch list. The highest legal authorities in the land were involved. One of the myths that has been allowed to perpetuate is that they [the police] were a bunch of mavericks. They were fully monitored at higher levels."

Not surprisingly, the Met refused to comment on an 'ongoing case'.

The story went on to say that Napper had been taken in for questioning, one month after Rachel's murder, on suspicion of the Green Chain attacks following a tip-off from a neighbour. But he was released after persuading detectives they had the wrong man. He offered to give a blood sample, which would have determined his guilt, but failed to attend and was never chased up on it.

It described the controversy over handling of the Nickell inquiry, and the fallout for many on the case. Lizzie was said to have received £200,000 for stress and depression, and left the force in 1998. Britton was reported as finding it difficult to deal with the criticism. Apparently he wanted to put his side of events long ago, but was told by the Met to remain silent.

But he insisted he would have done little to change what he regarded as "ground-breaking use" of psychological profiling. He added: "It's a tough world and it was all most unpleasant, but what I can never get away from is what the poor Nickell family will have to go through for the rest of their lives."

In his opinion, the government should set up an accredited list of official psychological profilers to bring their image out of the realms of "witchcraft and mysticism". But he had no desire to be on the list.

I was glad to hear that.

Apart from the failure to seek comments from Pedder, there are some glaring inaccuracies in the *Independent on Sunday* piece. I was acquitted in '94, not '93. Lizzie James received a well-publicised £125,000, not £200,000. Britton was not cleared after "an eight-year inquiry" – he managed to postpone the inquiry for eight years, until the BPS ruled it out of time. Neither was I ever in line for £500,000 compensation.

Keith Pedder is understandably furious at this distortion, damning Britton's version of events. "It's ridiculous. He's had a complete memory lapse. The whole purpose of our visit to the Plumstead murder inquiry was to establish if there was a link with Rachel's killing.

"Paul told me categorically there wasn't. In his words, 'the demons which motivated the attacker in each case were different.'

"Had he said they were connected I would have taken immediate action. I would have been failing in my duty not to have done so.

"When Mr Napper was subsequently arrested the following May we obviously looked at him for Rachel's murder, but he appeared to have a solid alibi. Only much later was it discovered that his work sheets for that week were missing.

"I am also surprised at Paul saying he was unhappy with the

Lizzie James letters. After all, he was the expert. They were part of his grand design. He planned every aspect. It was his opinion that mattered, not our gut feelings.

"He analysed each one of Stagg's letters and gave us an outline of what to write in reply. The words may have been ours but the content was his, every step of the way.

"He did the same for the tapes of Stagg's phone calls and his meetings with Lizzie, using their content to help craft the next letter. "

It was a self-serving betrayal of Pedder and the rest of the murder squad. And his words are so easily disproved. You only have to read page 394 of Britton's own book, *The Jigsaw Man*, where he describes how he was invited to profile the killer of Samantha and Jazmine. At the outset he was asked to consider whether the same man had murdered Rachel. Both women were blonde, attractive young mothers, both savagely attacked. In each case a child had been present, and a knife had been the murder weapon. But Britton rejected the similarities.

He wrote: "In my view the presence of a child in both attacks was the single largest differentiating factor between them, rather than a link.

"In the first case Alex was entirely a matter of disinterest to the killer, while Jazmine had been an important object of sexual gratification for the killer."

He regarded the Plumstead murders as a "much more refined scenario". In his view the killer gained far more pleasure from inflicting the post-mortem wounds than from the murder itself.

"There was a sense of exploration and discovery, whereas Rachel's murder had been frenzied and over within six minutes as the killer downloaded his anger and bitterness. It was a completely different scenario."

That's plain enough. *Britton said there was no connection whatsoever.*

On page 263, after he agrees to oversee the plan, Pedder asks him, "'How would it work specifically?'

"Using a white board I outlined two hypothetical covert operations designed to exploit the powerful deviant psychosexual functioning of Rachel's killer

"Let's assume that communication is established – based on a chance meeting or perhaps an exchange of letters for example."

Then Britton develops the letter-writing idea as one of two ways to contact me. On page 264 he writes, "This isn't for intellectual stimulation, it's his most powerful aid to masturbation. 'And this can be done by letter?' asked Pedder, referring to the operation using a female officer.

"In the initial stages Yes, but the murderer would quickly want to try to progress the relationship from written correspondence to personal meetings and an intimate relationship."

His ridiculous claim that his advice could have prevented all three murders is given the lie on page 274. Writing about the hunt for a serial rapist in the Eltham area, tellingly "a dozen miles from Wimbledon Common", he goes on: "The operation, code-named Ecclestone, had been running for a fortnight when Detective Inspector John Pearse called me in early September.

"After several postponed appointments and a horror drive around the M25 we finally met on a Wednesday afternoon in mid-September."

So by the time he was involved in the Green Chain investigation Rachel had been dead for two months! And yet he now claims that he might have prevented her death.

But there was one attack to which he strangely didn't seem to attach any significance. On pages 278 and 279 he describes the savage rape of a young blonde, pushing her two-year-old daughter in a buggy along a well-used path called King John's Path at Eltham – on the Green Chain route – on Bank

Holiday Sunday, May 24th 1992, less than two months before Rachel's murder.

The woman was stripped, beaten and sexually assaulted. She was left, writes Britton, "Looking like a bloody rag doll. Later she told police, 'I asked him not to kill me. He didn't stop hitting me. He put a rope around my neck and kept bashing me on the head.'

"Pearse took a sip of coffee and muttered, 'Brazen bastard. It was broad daylight on a busy footpath; anyone could have along.' 'He's a risk-taker — at least for the moment, I said.'"

Didn't that scenario — a young, blonde mother and small child, savagely attacked on a well-used path in broad daylight — later ring any bells? It could have been a dummy run for the Nickell attack, yet he didn't appear to notice any possible connection!

The only inarguable truth in his account was that the Bissett deaths might have been prevented. But not on account of his own advice. Acting on a neighbour's suspicions, Napper was stopped in the street by two detectives in respect of one of the Green Chain rapes.

He was a low-priority suspect and his height — six foot two — was much taller than the witness's description. There was also a six-month delay in taking him down for the murders. By a freak chance, his fingerprints were an almost identical match to Samantha Bissett's. It was only when prints taken from the murder scene were re-examined that one of them was found to belong to Napper.

A search of his home revealed a trainer print which exactly matched a bloody footprint found in the victims' flat. DNA tests immediately linked him to the Green Chain rapes, and he was identified by two of his victims at identity parades.

Luckily for me though, I'd never expected Napper becoming the new prime suspect for Rachel's murder to rehabilitate me. So I wasn't disappointed.

Although there was an initial softening of Fleet Street's biased attitude, they were soon up to their old tricks. The day after news of Napper's involvement broke, I was placed under media siege for quotes. The *Mail* started banging on my door at 8am. But the paper had consistently denigrated me, so I chose to speak exclusively to *The Sun*.

This piqued the *Mail*. Acting on the premise that I'd be too happy to object to what they wrote, they invented a couple of lines, then tacked on more words gleaned from old cuttings. The result was a first edition banner headline that read, 'STAGG: NOW I WANT £1 MILLION' across two pages. "'I'm entitled to every penny I can get,' he said yesterday. 'My life was ruined by a false accusation which was never proved by anybody. Now it has been proved to be a complete lie.'"

That was one of their supposed quotes. But then the right-hand page was filled with a comment piece that showed their utter contempt for me: 'PAYDAY FOR THE VIOLENT ODDBALL WITH A TASTE FOR KINKY SEX AND KNIVES'.

It included these patronising and insensitive remarks, "Strangely it is 41-year-old Stagg, more than anyone else, who refuses to move and put this dreadful chapter of his life behind him. He could have moved abroad or even moved house." This showed a complete lack of understanding of my situation and the real world I inhabit. Not surprisingly, it was written by some Sloane Ranger type. Her article was also full of careless inaccuracies about me and my home that seemed designed to denigrate me.

Their main story had a funny knock-on effect. When the first editions of *The Sun* landed on the *Mail*'s newsdesk, there was no mention of me wanting any money. That gave them second thoughts. They changed their main headline to read, 'STAGG: IN

LINE FOR £1 MILLION', giving it a whole new meaning, and they removed the "I'm entitled to every penny I can get" quote too!

But it didn't stop there. In an absurd about-turn, *The Sun* read their rival's headline and quotes and felt hard done by. So they incorporated the *Mail*'s manufactured words into what had been a very accurate interview, in their later editions.

You couldn't make it up – unless you worked for newspapers.

What later transpired about Napper's identification wasn't so funny for me, or the Nickell family. For it seems he should have been identified as the likely killer three years earlier.

Forensic scientists, carrying out a review of the case in 2001, had made an appalling blunder. They failed to test the tiny DNA sample found on Rachel's body; had they done so they would have matched it to Napper's, which by that time was on the database. It should have meant less years of torment for everyone concerned.

But I wasn't surprised. The Nickell case carries a curse. Everything about it seems to have been tainted and flawed. Not that Napper's DNA identification has made much difference to me either way. Three years after, I'm still in limbo and still under public suspicion.

Hate mail still arrives occasionally. So too the sly looks and muttered curses. People still regard me as suspect, and my job prospects remain at zero.

There *has* been a change in the press attitude, which generally seems more inclined to acknowledge my innocence. But predictably, not all the coverage is good. And even the good ones can give me a backhander. Boris Johnson wrote a very sympathetic piece about me in the *Daily Telegraph*, but spoilt it by referring to my "dodgy-looking singlets" and "malodorous flat".

(But fair play to the old bumbler. He did send me a very gracious handwritten apology when I complained. No other writer has ever done that.)

But similar descriptions have become commonplace. They have simply moved the angle of their attack. Now, it appears, I was such an unsavoury creature that I *deserved* all the bad things that happened to me. I am, variously, an oddball, misfit, jobless, violent, loner with a sordid, kinky sex and black magic-filled past who lives in the squalor of a black-painted flat, festooned with knives, on a sinkhole council estate!

Ever since the erroneous *Daily Mirror* headline, 'Now I'll Make A Killing', at the end of my trial, the papers have been obsessed with the payouts I'm supposed to have been getting. A £1million compensation figure has always been their favourite (although £500,000, and latterly £250,000, have made regular appearances). It gives them grounds to add greedy, grasping, money-grubbing and avaricious to their anti-Stagg lexicon.

I have *never* spoken of any specific figures to anyone, friend, family or journalist. Money was never the main object of my actions against the Met and Paul Britton. What I wanted most of all was some sort of apology, or an acknowledgement that they did me wrong.

That would have gone so much further than any monetary award in clearing me in the public's mind. It was my good name that I wanted back. In any case, I've always been highly sceptical about these vast sums that I'm supposed to have been getting.

This Home Office award is a typical case in point. No set figure has ever been mentioned in the official correspondence. It is entirely up to the independent assessor, and no one else. He could decide that I'm not entitled to a penny! That's something that no newspaper has bothered to point out.

Of course, money would be a help. I've got debts that I want to pay off, and it would be nice to have a few home comforts. The sort of things I could afford if I had a job. Sadly, I don't think that's ever going to happen. My solicitor's failure to find a psychologist prepared to give me a simple examination is proof of that.

If intelligent professional people feel there is too much stigma attached to me, how likely is that prospective employers will take a different view? I seem doomed to the dole forever.

Having no job is almost as bad as being cast as the bogeyman hate-figure. But even the most menial positions have been denied me. For thirteen years now my search for proper work, full or part-time, has been relentless – and futile. I've lost count of the different jobs I've applied for, and always been rejected from.

Van driver, postman, meter reader, shop fitter, cleaner, dustman, even road-sweeper – all my applications were turned down, or even worse, ignored. The only exception was when a male escort firm took me on their books briefly – until they realised who I was.

It's soul-destroying for someone who needs to work as much for his self-respect as for the money. I'm still fit and strong at forty-four, although 'ageism' is probably my next obstacle to finding employment.

I've never been scared of hard work and I've developed a lot of odd-jobbing skills over the years. My home bears witness to this. I built my kitchen units from scratch, tiled the walls and the downstairs lavatory. In my living room I rebuilt the fireplace, and I've laid laminated flooring in the hall.

I'm currently replacing the banisters and putting a false ceiling above the stairwell, before moving on to completely refurbish the bathroom. The hardest job was building a steep flight of concrete steps down into the garden. If it all makes me sound like some DIY fanatic, I take a pride in my home, and it keeps me busy whenever I can afford the materials.

I inherited a love of growing things from my father, and the garden is full of flowers, nurtured from seeds and cuttings. Working among the blooms and plants is very soothing. And over the past year I've found another sort of peace, in developing a relationship with a very nice woman that, so far, is non-sexual.

Terri Marchant had been my brother Tony's girlfriend, so we had known each other as teenagers on the estate. After returning from America, she got in touch with me again and a close friendship developed. It did have one disturbing side effect, however: My stalker surfaced again. And she wasn't best pleased.

Somehow she obtained my mobile number and sent me hours of disturbing recorded messages and texts. One minute she was saying she loved me, the next she threatened to put bricks through my windows if I didn't give Terri up.

The threats against us got so bad that I changed my number and informed the police. I felt sorry for the woman, but she had become yet another nutter to fear. I had too many of those out to get me already. Terri was terrified, and we eventually managed to get a restraining order put on this woman. (If she breaks it she could go to prison. I don't want that to happen, but there doesn't seem to be any alternative.)

For the first time in my life I have a connection with a woman that isn't dependent on sex or booze. We kiss and cuddle, but that's as far as we go. I've come to the conclusion that I'm not really a sexual person. I like the idea of it more than the act. When you're young it's the be-all and end-all. But once you've had it, you find it's not all it's cracked up to be.

Now I'm older I find friendship and intimacy much more important, probably because I've felt deprived of these things for a lot of my life.

From the start I made it clear to Terri I would never get married again, and she understands. We have found a way of life that's good for both of us, by having our own time apart. Terri lives with her two youngest children, aged sixteen and four, in Farnham, twenty-odd miles away from me. They are great kids, and I feel they have come to love me. I really enjoy their company. They are a lovely family, and I settle in comfortably whenever I'm there – which is sometimes as long as two or three weeks at a time.

Bearing mind that I've been single for most of my life, I've become a bit selfish and I'm still learning to adjust to other people's needs. Terri understands this, and assures me she is fine with the way things are going. We have even discussed the possibility that, one day, we might settle down together permanently.

Luckily, we think of each other as soulmates and share a sense of humour. Laughter is something that's been missing from my life. We enjoy going for walks with the kids in the countryside near her home. I've even taken them on days out to the seaside – the kind of ordinary things that I'd forgotten about – although I'm still uncomfortable in crowds.

Neither of us feels the need to go out to pubs or restaurants – not that we can afford to. We prefer to stay home and watch television. It may sound boring, but it's safe. In some respects, staying with Terri is like a holiday for me.

Back home in Roehampton, the realities of life come home to me and my siege mentality takes hold once again.

The strain of always being on my guard. Those fruitless journeys to the Job Centre. The strangers' scowls, or the dawning recognition.

Perhaps things will change. If the CPS does charge Robert Napper with Rachel's murder, it will go a long way toward vindicating me. I'll take the Home Office award as the apology the Met will probably never give me. But if it doesn't happen, I'll live with it.

I'm going to travel in hope and prepare for disappointment – just like the AA's motto, "One day at a time."

To some I will always be 'the man who got away with murder'. But all I ever can be is a man who got on with his life – whatever that might entail.